Land of Muscovy

By E. M. Almedingen

KATIA
YOUNG MARK
A CANDLE AT DUSK
FANNY
ELLEN
ANNA
LAND OF MUSCOVY

E. M. Almedingen

LAND
OF
MUSCOVY

The History of Early Russia

ILLUSTRATED BY MICHAEL CHARLTON

FARRAR, STRAUS and GIROUX | NEW YORK

Land of Muscovy

Chapter 1

The opening of the story is all movement. Sometime between A.D. 400 and 600 innumerable nomadic Slav tribes, who descended from the Scythians, decided to enlarge their wanderings. Some among them made for the vast steppe country in the deep south of present Russia. Others went up north, reached what would later be called the central plain, and made rough settlements there near a lake or along the bank of some river. The land was rich and abundant. It pleased them and was theirs for the taking. Keen hunters, they found the forests teeming with animals to provide food and clothing. Trees they had not known yielded nuts and fruit. Indigenous seeds, sprouting from the bountiful soil, proved edible. As to lakes and rivers, they were incredibly rich in fish. Altogether the several Slav tribes thought themselves in paradise.

They were not isolated. Living on the banks of great waterways which linked Scandinavia to Byzantium, the Slavs would meet Danes, Norsemen, and Swedes. By A.D. 800 they had learned to trade the great surplus of their land's bounty with the foreigners. In the summer, when the Scandinavian ships sailed down to the south, the Slavs had hides, timber, wax, and much else to barter for what they needed: iron ore, salt, weapons from Norwegian and Swedish smithies, and stone slabs.

The settlers were kept busy and all would have gone well with them had it not been for their lack of cohesion. They seemed to spend what leisure they had in fighting one another. Inter-tribal feuds, invariably breaking into bloodshed, grew into a matter of honor with the Slavs. A quarrel over the carcass of a wild boar would start a fight between two men and then spread into a battle among the tribes.

However, there came moments of comparative quiet, and the tribes would get together and hold a primitive parliament known in Old Slavonic as *viéche*. Since the Slavs were illiterate, no records of such gatherings have reached us—with one exception, partly historical, partly legendary. The story was recorded centuries later by a chronicler in whose mind fact and fantasy were woven together into a beautiful tapestry.

Some time in the mid-ninth century a few Slavs at a *vieche* persuaded their countrymen to send an embassy to the Swedish tribe of Rus. The message had

4

to be verbal: "Our lands are big and bountiful, yet there is no order among us. Come and rule over us."

The embassy may well be legendary, but it is history that chieftains from Sweden came and moored their ships on the banks of the West Dvina and the Dnieper. The greatest among them was one Rurik, and Kiev became the capital of his principality. Others went to Novgorod and Pskov. At last the Slav tribes became one nation. Their country became known as Rus, and the date A.D. 862, whether rightly or wrongly, denoted the beginning of Russia. The Swedish chieftains brought many followers and the Scandinavian blood was mingled with that of the Slavs.

Rurik founded a dynasty which lasted for over seven centuries. Little by little, various principalities sprang up: Sousdal, Yaroslavl, Riazan, Tver, Vladimir, and many others. But Kiev on the banks of the Dnieper remained a focal point, a city famous for its lovely buildings, its expanding trade, its wise princes, and the ever increasing cultural and social links with the West and Byzantium. Rus became Christian at the end of the ninth century, when Vladimir of Kiev married a Greek princess. Later, daughters of the Rurik dynasty married kings of Norway, Bohemia, and Hungary. One became the wife of Henry I of France. Another wedded the Emperor Henry IV.

Gone were the primitive, savage days. Rus had an alphabet and a lovely, fluent language. Scholars crowded into Kiev, where schools and libraries were

5

founded, and architects from Italy and Greece directed the building of many churches. Elsewhere, each principality, sharing the Kiev culture, was governed by a prince together with his *dúma*, an assembly of princely descendants of Rurik and of *boyárs*, the untitled landowners. But the humblest plowman had the right of access to his prince.

In these days Rus never went to war with any country in the West. Her only enemies were the still-savage nomadic tribes from the deep south.

It was the law of succession which proved the undoing of Rus. On the death of a prince, all his lands had to be parceled out among his sons, and that opened the way to endless dissensions, the heirs quarreling and killing one another for a small town, a forest, a river. Trade suffered, except at Novgorod and Pskov. Schools were neglected. Men began to prefer weapons to books. Peasants, their harvests destroyed in battles, felt bewildered and bereft.

For nearly two hundred years that strife went on, weakening one principality after another. Early in the thirteenth century enormous Tartar hordes, led by Khan Batiy, crossed the Volga. Rus had neither unity nor strength to resist the invader. Within a few years the whole vast land lay under the Tartar yoke. Such was their power that they erected something of an iron curtain between Rus and the West. Novgorod, spared the sack but put under tribute, alone continued its trade with the Germans and the south.

The Tartar domination continued until in 1380 a prince mustered an army and defeated them at Kulikovo. The victory did not crush the yoke altogether but the people were heartened, and Dimitry Donskoy, Prince of Moscow and a member of the ancient house of Rurik, became a national hero.

He freed the fortress of Moscow from Tartar rule, and a new city grew up which replaced Kiev as the center of Russia. Dimitry's successors were men of vision and cunning. One of them was wealthy enough to buy land from the Tartars. One by one, the smaller principalities found themselves belonging to Moscow. Their rulers were glad to shed responsibility. The lesser folk were left to accept the inevitable. By the fifteenth century, with the exception of "free Novgorod," the unification was complete under Ivan III, and Rus became Muscovy. The ancient house of Rurik, ruling within the white-walled Kremlin, seemed invincible. Foreign embassies began coming to Moscow, and foreign architects and artists worked for Ivan's pleasure. Trade expanded and the treasury was full—though, away from Moscow, the peasantry still eked a scant livelihood in squalor, dirt, utter ignorance, and constant dread of tax collectors from Moscow. Ivan III was a strong ruler. Yet he needed money, especially for his constant wars with Poland, Livonia, Lithuania, and the Crimean Tartars, and merchants and peasants were heavily taxed.

The ghosts of old Kiev would not have recognized much affinity between Rus and Muscovy. Ivan III was a czar in all but name, and Rus had never before known autocracy. The people of Rus from the noblest boyar or landowner down to the poorest peasant had kept their independence. A man owning no more than a cow and a couple of hens had been free to enter his prince's palace and lay his grievance before him.

An unpleasing leaven was left by the Tartar yoke. Servility, expressed by prostrations and deep obeisances, crept into all levels of life. People had grown used to fear and the habit would not be uprooted. Fear of the Prince of Moscow, his councilors, his judges, and, above all, his tax collectors entered the Muscovite pattern. In old Rus they would have laughed at the posturings in Moscow. The princes of Kiev had feasted, sung, laughed, and danced with their friends, the women joining in the merriment. In Moscow, the Prince ate alone, served by kneeling lackeys. He gave formal audiences, his scarlet-draped throne surrounded by courtiers, and no woman ever appeared at those functions.

That was yet another legacy of the Tartar yoke. Peasant women were untouched by it, since in those days few, if any, country folk left their native villages. But in the cities and particularly in Moscow, boyars' wives and other women of rank led cloistered lives. They occupied part of the house, known as *terem*, where no man might go. They were surrounded by women servants. Occasionally they attended a service at some church or went on a pilgrimage to the nearest convent. Whether they rode or walked, their faces were veiled. In the *terem* they spent their days occupied with embroidery, gossip, watching a female dwarf's pranks, eating and singing. Dancing was forbidden. Husbands and fathers were the only constellations on their horizon. Girls' marriages were arranged by the respective fathers, and the bride would first meet her groom when facing the priest before the service began. Once married, she was not her own mistress. If she had sons, they stayed with her for four or five years and then left their nurses and the *terem* forever. Women had been chattels to the Tartars, and even in the merchant households women were now considered chattels in Muscovy. The Kiev ladies had

9

been able to read and write in Greek and Old Slavonic. The Muscovite women, on the other hand, were illiterate; there were no books in the *terem*.

Muscovy waxed rich. In consequence, its economic pattern grew more and more complicated. Taxation became an imperative. Princes of Rurik descent, boyars, merchants, and town artisans paid taxes in land, money, or goods. Peasants were taxed in kind since they had no money. Muscovite tax collectors swooped down like locusts. The Grand Duke of Moscow needed money for his troops and his campaigns. To the peasant folk the names Livonia, Lithuania, Poland, the Crimean Tartars meant nothing, but they understood that they must part with some of their grain, linen woven by their women, and vegetables. Many among them were too poor to spare even a sack of grain. The land was rich, but forests and rivers belonged to secular and ecclesiastical overlords. Poaching carried grim penalties. Peasants lived on gruel, vegetables, rye bread, milk, and eggs if they were lucky. Their clothing was coarse and in winter most inadequate. There were hamlets where the headman was in custody of one pair of boots which were shared by the entire settlement. These conditions of the late fifteenth century were not to change much till the mid-nineteenth century. But at least the peasant women, unlike their city counterparts, could dance. They abandoned themselves to their few summer festivals with dancing and singing. Medical help they had none, but few were the villages without a *znakhár* ("knowing man") or his female counterpart, who eased, healed, and sometimes cursed with herbs and incantations.

The serfdom of later centuries did not exist, but many peasants, crushed by taxation, offered themselves in *kabála* to richer folk. This was, in fact, virtual serfdom, since they belonged to the person who accepted them as *kabálniky*. *Kabala* might last for a few years or a lifetime.

Little by little, those in the neighborhood of a wealthy abbey became *monastyrskie lundi*, "monks' people" living off the abbey. Wholly illiterate and ignorant, still they had plenty of mother wit and cunning. They did not expect any spiritual benefits from an abbey; they were pious by custom but their deeper allegiance stemmed from the pagan past, from which they got their love of color. They used the juice of whortleberries and cranberries to brighten hodden-gray shifts which their womenfolk spun through the long winters. Moscow was the end of the world to them, and they firmly believed that the earth was upheld by seven whales.

Chapter II

The first rulers of Muscovy regarded all foreigners with the suspicion inherited from the Tartars. Yet foreigners had their uses as architects, artisans, and soldiers. Moscow had once been a city of timber and thatch, because of the high cost of stone, but now, the little town having become a capital, high stone walls, palaces, and mansions were being built by "men of skill" from Italy and the Low Countries, and Ivan III appreciated their services. Other aliens followed, to work in metal, glass, dyes, leather. Yet any foreigner, however fine the work done by him, was regarded as an "offspring of Satan." A special quarter in the city was allotted to these immigrants, where they lived and had their workshops. The Muscovites banned all social interchange with them and many a Russian priest bemoaned their very presence in the "Orthodox city." No matter where these foreigners came from—Scotland, Flanders, England,

Italy, or France—they were known as *niemtzy.*
Niemoy means "dumb" in Russian, a language hard
for a foreigner to master.

In the fifteenth century the Muscovites, both nobles
and merchants, wore fur-hemmed gowns reaching
down to the ankles and grew long beards. They walked
sedately and kept their womenfolk in strict seclusion.
There were horrifying stories about foreign women,
their faces unveiled, sharing meals with their menfolk, who dressed in doublets, breeches, and hose;
about milk being drunk on fast days, a crime at that
time in the eyes of an Orthodox Christian; and, worst
of all, about a Dutch woman who knew how to read
and do her husband's accounts.

Moscow was a city no longer. She was a state, growing rich and important, and the jealousy of neighbors
led to frequent wars. Success and defeat followed one
another. The Muscovite army consisted of peasants,
poor boyars' and merchants' sons. They went to battle
on horseback. There was no infantry and hardly any
artillery. For weapons they had bows and arrows,
hatchets and pikes. Noblemen's sons alone had the
right to carry swords. The victualing of the army was
rather odd : the men were allowed porridge, ham, and
salt. Bread and vegetables were left to chance. Any
village along the way could be pillaged with impunity.

Muscovite trade would have expanded more quickly
if the country had had a sea outlet. But to the west lay
the Baltic, jealously guarded by Denmark and by the
German merchants of the Hansa. Down in the south,
the Black Sea was in the hands of the Turks and the

Crimean Tartars. The great Volga only ran down to the Caspian, a lake rather than a sea—and, anyway, its great ports, Kazan and Astrakhan, were in Tartar hands until the days of Ivan III's grandson. Hundreds of miles to the north of Moscow lay the White Sea, definitely within the Muscovite dominions but most inconveniently frozen for the better part of the year; and there were no passable roads northward past Tver.

Europe, flushed with the Renaissance, could not but feel curious about Muscovy. The Turks had crushed Byzantium in 1452. Twenty years later Ivan III of Muscovy married Princess Zoë Paleologue of that country. She went to her bridegroom with a train of Greek scholars in her retinue. It was a happy and enlightened fusion: the Byzantine idea entering the Muscovite mind, but the enlightenment stretched no farther than the capital. Greeks, who shared the Muscovites' faith, were welcomed, but casual travelers from across the border were not encouraged, and the aliens in the Prince's service were not permitted to roam at will over his domains. It seemed as though Muscovy, centuries behind Western culture, guarded some secret she would not share with outsiders. The idea propounded by a monk added much to Muscovite arrogance: "The first Rome fell; Byzantium was the second Rome, and it has fallen to the Turk. Moscow is the third Rome. There shall not be another."

Ivan III ruled in Moscow harshly but justly. The Princes of Moscow assumed the double eagle of Byzantium, but neither Ivan nor his son Vassily called themselves czars.

14

Chapter III

The chronicle tells us that Prince Vassily, son of Ivan III, would not have his wife and his two sons near his deathbed. Ivan, the elder boy, then in his fourth year, and George, his brother, a delicate infant of two, were still in the *terem*, with their nurses and the ladies in attendance on their mother. When the news of Vassily's death winged over the palace, the widow, Elena Glynskaya, weeping and wringing her hands, knelt before Ivan, kissed his hands and the hem of his smock, calling him her lord, son, and sovereign. All the women present followed her example. Ivan, now Ivan IV, Prince of Muscovy, understood nothing, yet good manners demanded that he should join in the sobbing and weeping. Then men came in and served a meal on bended knee.

His bewilderment grew apace the next day. They woke him early and dressed him in clothes he had never worn before: silver-embroidered boots, a heavy brocade gown reaching down to the ankles, an embroidered crimson velvet cape to his waist, a heavy gold chain on his breast, and silver-threaded white gauntlets on his hands. He was taken out of the *terem* and led into one of the Kremlin cathedrals, where the Metropolitan, the entire hierarchy behind him, blessed him and named him the rightful prince and sovereign of the whole of Muscovy. The ceremony over, he was led back to the *terem*, the women relieved him of the heavy clothes, and he happily ate a plate of raisin porridge and played with his little brother. He did not know that messengers from Muscovy had ridden far and wide to proclaim his accession. It pleased him to remain in the *terem*, but it irked him to see people kneeling to him and to submit to the women thrusting the ceremonial clothes on him. The child was led to the audience hall, the courtiers crowding around him. He was placed on a velvet-cushioned throne and listened to formal speeches of men from Sweden, Lithuania, Livonia, Poland, and beyond. He was too small to follow their trend. His tutors answered for him. He could only smile. He knew nothing of politics, and there was nobody to tell him that Lithuania, for one, hoped to conquer Moscovy, its ruler being a mere child and its regent a weak woman, unpopular among the nobility and unknown to the common people.

Ivan's mother, Elena, was regent, but being a woman, she wielded no real authority. The govern-

ment, both clerical and lay, made all the decisions necessary for strengthening the fair inheritance left by Vassily. Trade flourished. Muscovite markets grew in number and importance. At the Kremlin, Ivan's *dvor*, or household, consisted of noblemen who ruled over a huge number of underlings, cooks, scullions, butlers, footmen, men of the bodyguard, locksmiths, architects, shoemakers, tailors, monks to organize pilgrimages, and men of cunning whose sole duty was to make "diverting toys" and to provide entertainment for Ivan.

Muscovy made peace with Sweden when Ivan was

seven, but trouble soon broke out with the turbulent Khan of Kazan on the east bank of the Volga and with the Crimean Tartars farther to the south. Both the Livonian and the Polish embassies were pleased and reported back that there was no real ruler in Muscovy. The regent was a figurehead, as was her little son, and the power was being disputed by several factions among the nobility. Such a country, argued foreign ambassadors, would not be difficult to subdue. The Shuyskie princes, a clan of Rurik descent, were prominent at the time, and Elena was afraid of them. Little by little, these men made themselves virtual governors of Ivan and surrounded him by intimates who encouraged the latent cruelty in the child. They clapped their hands whenever they saw Ivan's vicious treatment of horses and pets. The Shuyskies' sycophants laughed themselves to tears when their little sovereign pinched, scratched, and struck an unfortunate footman for bringing a silver platter instead of a gold one. They assured Ivan that he was developing well and they showered him with "rewards" stolen by them from his own treasury.

In the late spring of 1538 Elena died, and rumors flew all over Europe: the Princess Dowager had been poisoned by orders of a Prince Shuyskie. Nobody could tell if such stories were genuine but it was true that the several factions nearest to the throne came to the forefront, and Ivan's household was changed almost overnight.

Ceremonial prostrations, respect mingled with

18

shameless servility, the rich garments of brocade and the gold crown—all this was so much window dressing in the audience hall to convince the foreign ambassadors that Prince Ivan IV, for all that he was an eight-year-old boy, remained an autocrat, surrounded by the splendors of his rank, whose very whims, let alone his will, were law.

But the boy's mind had not been wholly corrupted by the bad influences around him. He knew that the dazzling ceremonies in the audience hall were so many pretenses; he knew that, once he was back in his own apartments, the heavy robes of state would not be taken off his shoulders with the courtesy due to his rank. In the sight of foreigners, Ivan was an autocrat. To the household, among whom he had not a single close friend, he was a mere nuisance of a boy. Prince Ivan Shuyskie and his sycophants invaded Ivan's rooms without leave, sprawled on benches, spat on the floor, and swore at Ivan. Prince Shuyskie mocked at Ivan's parents, whose memory was very dear to the boy. He said that Vassily, a man of straw, had been unfit to govern and that Elena was born a fool. On one occasion, Shuyskie snatched a scarf that had belonged to Elena, tore it up, and then trampled on the pieces.

There were other indignities and privations. Ivan and his little brother had been used to delicate food at dinner and supper, and had had their shirts and drawers changed every day. Now, all decency and tidiness tossed to the winds, the boys were lucky to have some sour milk, a little dry rye bread, and a pickled herring for their daily meal. When Ivan asked for apples and a bowl of hot broth on a very cold day, he was answered with a shrug and a smirk. The boys' linen was dirty, their shoes all but worn out, their coats far shabbier than those worn by a merchant's son. The finery, kept in coffers and chests, was rigidly preserved for state occasions, and these were not very many. Again and again the Prince's guardians would hold a reception and announce that their young sovereign was not well enough to make an appearance.

Undernourished, unkempt, uncared for, the two boys suffered much from cold. Moscow winters were grim. The houses were heated with big porcelain stoves stoked with logs. In the Kremlin Palace these stoves were never supposed to go out. But contrary instructions must have been given and seldom were the great baskets full of logs. On at least one occasion when a particularly severe winter held Moscow in its iron grip, the great stove in the common room remained cold and the little Princes were told to spend the day in their small bedroom. Their guardians, the Princes Shuyskie, being busy with governmental matters, were to make no visits that day and so no heating was to be wasted.

Far worse incidents darkened Ivan's childhood.

There were some in the household whose hearts were touched by compassion for the boys. Extra coverlets, clean linen, apples, gingerbread, and nuts would be smuggled into the apartments, and the sorry nag assigned to Ivan would be replaced by a decent mount. When the guardians and their hangers-on left the boys, those intrepid comforters would tiptoe in and lighten an hour or so by telling fairy tales or fragments of old Muscovite stories.

One evening, Ivan, who was then about ten, was falling asleep. The two or three friendly folk had just put out the candles, left the light burning in front of the ikon corner, and moved to the door when loud oaths and the clang of swords broke out in the adjoining room. Shuyskie and his gang burst into the bedroom, candles were brought in, and the friends were knocked down, shouts of "treason" deafening their cries for mercy. Shuyskie's sycophants unsheathed their swords. Ivan leaped out of bed, sobbing, and begged the murderers to be merciful. Nobody listened to him. The butchers having finished their work, the bodies were dragged out and thrown down the stairs. Prince Shuyskie came back to tell the horror-struck child that justice had been done : those men had plotted to worm their way into Ivan's favor, to poison him in the end, and to elect one of themselves as the sovereign of Muscovy.

Ivan believed none of it, but that dreadful night left a mark never to be forgotten. The blood so cruelly shed in his bedroom led to the birth of a new era in Muscovite history. The crime was responsible for a new hatred and contempt in the boy toward the ancient noble houses. Ivan saw them all as enemies. He brooded over his inherited rights now denied him, he learned to dissemble his grief and anger, and the idea crept into his mind of a fearful struggle to come.

We cannot tell how soon Ivan learned his letters,

but his early teens found him absorbed in books and maps. He mastered Latin, Greek, the early history of his country, and geography. He learned the extent of his great dominions and he reminded himself that the years of his vassalage were drawing to an end: as the law stood, he would be of age on his sixteenth birthday.

Brilliantly gifted, Ivan grasped matters and solved problems few boys of his age could have grappled with. At formal audiences he still gave answers that had been dictated by his guardians, but he was no longer a sumptuously dressed figurehead. He listened to ambassadorial speeches, but interpreter's services were now not necessary. Ivan knew his Latin and understood every word.

Little by little, his earlier submissiveness began to evaporate. Tall for his age, his eyes flashing anger at the least disservice, Ivan no longer asked for this or that: he gave orders and his manner was so assured that the household, however reluctantly, began to obey. The Shuyskie clan, quick to observe the change, remembered that Ivan's coming of age was no longer distant, and changed their manner. Ivan treated them politely but distantly.

In his fourteenth year the Prince asserted himself for the first time in the crowded throne hall. The ambassador of the Holy Roman Empire was being received in formal audience. The preliminary courtesies over, the ambassador started his speech. The matter concerned Livonia. The gentleman, whose master the

Emperor was anxious for hostilities to cease, spoke eloquently about the advantages likely to fall to Muscovy once a truce was signed. When he finished, the court interpreter knelt before the throne and asked for leave to begin his task. From the crimson-draped throne Ivan's voice was heard telling the interpreter that his services were not needed. In slow and careful Latin the Prince replied to the ambassador. Muscovy's answer would be given as soon as he, the sovereign, had consulted the Duma.

Ivan was no longer a child. From books and maps he turned his attention to governmental matters. He acquainted himself with details of lay and ecclesiastical government. Taxation, exports and imports, trade, the condition of the army, merchantry, and peasantry —nothing escaped Ivan. He asked pertinent questions. He scanned the ledgers. At the sittings of the Duma, he no longer assented to every decision made by the 150 members of the nobility. He questioned minutely, he reflected, and either approved or rejected the nobility's suggestions. For his holidays Ivan left the Kremlin for some neighborhood monastery or else rode out of Moscow into its environs, his mount accoutered as befitted his rank, his bodyguard of grooms and soldiers wholly won over by his courtesy and benevolence.

From one poor village to another, Ivan would ride, learning about his people, the illiterate, downtrodden, hard-worked, and cheerful common folk of Muscovy. Ivan sensed that their rapturous greetings were genuine, that they reverenced his rank, and had no fear of him. When he dismounted, the peasants knelt to greet him, kissing his knees and hands—but these expressions came from affection, not from servility. They did not come empty-handed: they would bring cranberries, a *karaváy* (round, flat loaf of rye), flowers, a few eggs, a basket plaited from birch bast by the women, a bunch of turnips, or a handful of apples; and Ivan accepted everything with a smile. There were also grievances: a fire, a bad harvest, some pest smiting at what few fowls they had, a complaint about a heartless landlord or a cruel tax collector. Ivan, whose memory was miraculous, took in all the details, not a single note written down.

He felt himself at home among his people. He saw them as a strong wall between himself and the self-seeking sycophants to whom sincerity of speech and action was about as familiar as the Chinese alphabet. Ivan, riding back to Moscow, thought that those illiterate common folk were the very sinews of Muscovy.

Chapter IV

From north to south, Muscovy was beautiful. She had no hills, but there were lovely wide rivers, the Dvina, the Volga, the Oka, and the Don. Deep forests, chiefly of fir, birch, and elm, suggested so many dark green islands up and down the apparently shoreless and more lightly colored sea of pasture and arable land, streaked here and there by the silver blue of water from the rivers' numberless tributaries. A special office in Moscow had the upkeep of roads in its care, and by the sixteenth century Muscovy had post horses for hire, harnessed to rather primitive carriages and driven by men known as *yamchiky*.

But neither the capital nor any of the lesser cities contained much that was beautiful, except for some churches designed by foreigners in Muscovite service. In Moscow, the Kremlin alone had palaces, churches, and government buildings of stone. Elsewhere, even noblemen's houses were of timber, usually fir, the planks held together by tar. Roofs were made of shingle and covered with moss. In the very neighborhood of the Kremlin, streets were unpaved. Even the mansions of wealthy boyars were not glazed, but the narrow windows had sheets of finely flaked, transparent *sluda*, a soft mineral substance found along the banks of the north Dvina and elsewhere. For staircases there were timbered ladders. Houses were heated with enormous stoves fed by logs. Wooden benches were built all around the walls. The east corner of every room was known as the "red corner." Family ikons hung there, tier upon tier, and tiny silver-gilt bowls, inlaid with glass and filled with oil, carrying homemade wicks, would burn there day and night in honor of the Trinity, the Lord's Mother, and whatever saints were preferred by the household. Inherited silver and gold plate, used only on important occasions, stood on shelves in another corner. For comfort and color, there were cushions, rugs, and carpets, the last in particular looking like a rainbow of multicolored wool, either home-woven or made in Persia and India and purchased from foreign merchants. You reached the most important room through a stoutly timbered *seny*, a kind of roofed-in porch in front of the house.

Sanitation did not exist, but the Muscovites were, on the whole, clean. Behind the kitchens of any well-to-do family stood a low-roofed building, called *bány*, the interior divided into three parts, furnished with long benches and huge wooden tubs for water, each room with a great stove. The middle one was used for washing. The men of the family would lie flat on the benches; servants poured tubfuls of hot water over them and rubbed them with soap made of animal fat mixed with linseed oil and other ingredients. That finished, the men, still naked, passed into the third room, which was full of steam. There they lay and sweated until breath failed them, and servants supported them into the first room, very warm but not unbearably so, where the men could lie and have cooling drinks brought to them, generally great goblets of *kvass*, a national drink made of rye bread, raspberries, or some other fruit. A visit to the *bany* was a weekly occasion. The females of the household also had their appointed bathing hours. The Muscovites were extremely pious and visits to the *bany* would take place on the eve of every important feast.

Conditions were wholly different in the countryside. A peasant's home was a one-roomed hut, often with not a single window to it, the floor consisting of soil. There would be a stove to warm the inhabitants and for them to cook on. In place of the gilded and bejeweled "red corner" of noblemen and merchants, peasants would have a single ikon, and they could not always afford the oil for the little lamp. They were fortunate if they had rough sheepskins to cover the benches. They had no other furniture. In that one room they lived, ate, slept, and worked through the long winter evenings. In place of the candles of wax and tallow used by their betters, the peasants had *luchíny*, a branch of elm or birch dipped into fat and lit from the fire in the stove. A *luchina* gave a flickering and uncertain light, but that in no way interfered with their work. The men made trugs, baskets, sandals, and fishing rods.

A hamlet might or might not have a communal *bany* shed, but the peasantry cared little for cleanliness through the long wintry months. In the spring, the women would make for the nearest stream or river for the annual clothes wash. They would beat the dirt and sweat out of the garments with long wooden sticks. Soap had no room in their budget.

The nobles wore tall, bejeweled hats and fur-trimmed velvet gowns falling down to their ankles, with boots of red or yellow leather. Merchants' hats were not as tall and they were not embellished with jewels. Their gowns reached down to the ankles too, but they were of cloth, usually dark blue, and the boots were black. In the winter, the peasants wore loose gowns made of whatever wool was handy. There were instances of hamlets sharing two pairs of boots among thirty men—because leather was expensive. In the summer, peasants wore smocks that reached down to the knees, and homemade bast sandals. Their children, kept indoors all through the winter, ran about barefoot in homemade, sleeveless shirts reaching to the knees. The ladies in Moscow had velvet, brocade, and silk garments in their coffers, and finely woven lawn to wear in the summer. The peasant women were proud of their homespun, home-dyed blue, green, and red loose blouses, skirts, and aprons. All the men, from nobleman to peasant, were bearded, though the former used ivory combs and the latter wore his beard raveled to the extreme.

There was also a sharp difference in the diet between town and country. No Muscovite, high or low, considered breakfast a meal. The day was begun with a mug of mead, kvass, or milk. Everyone had two meals a day : dinner and supper. At the Kremlin Palace and in noblemen's mansions, the dinner might begin at noon and last three or four hours when there were guests. Supper was a much smaller meal. The upper classes were most indulgent in the matter of imported spices, pepper, nutmeg, coriander, and cinnamon. Big saltcellars and jugs of vinegar stood on the table, which would be covered with a fine white cloth. They used knives and spoons and mopped up some particularly exciting sauce with bread. Being very pious, the Muscovites made the sign of the cross before they used a knife or broke a piece of bread.

Muscovy supplied abundant victuals. Lakes and rivers teemed with most succulent fish—sturgeon, salmon, trout, carp, and pike. White salmon was a great favorite. Imported lemons and oranges were pickled and served with fish and meat. For the rest, they had beef and pork, poultry and game, all home reared. For dessert they might have apples, nuts, or small sweet turnips. They drank kvass, honey mead, and water: milk was known as a woman's tipple. There were no vineyards in Muscovy. Foreign wines were highly taxed and appeared on special occasions only, but the wealthy Muscovites could and did get drunk on very potent honey mead. Indeed, drunkenness early became Muscovy's curse.

No animal food, not even milk, butter, and eggs, was allowed during the four great fasts of the year. The hierarchy saw to it that the law was observed. But fasting had nothing to do with the quantity of food eaten: huge fish and gigantic pastries, stuffed with cabbage or mushrooms, were within the law. The Muscovites liked to point out that their enormous diet was due to the climate. "Cold sharpens hunger," they said—but the argument could not hold through the hot Muscovite summers. Merchants, if it is possible, ate even more liberally than nobles. On one merchant's feast day—that is, the day of his saint's commemoration—at Tver, some distance north of Moscow, the cooks boiled, baked, and fried for twenty-four hours, and the festal dinner consisted of thirty-eight courses.

Abundance flowed like a river in full spate up and down Muscovy, but the peasantry had little share in this luxury even though they spent their lives in the heart of it. The yield of field, meadow, forest, and river was controlled most strictly. The peasant plowed, sowed, and harvested, but the rye, oats, and barley

30

were not all his: there was the parish priest's tithe, and the landlord claimed his share. A neighboring monastery demanded payment in kind for all grain ground at the monastery mill. What root vegetables the peasant sowed in his patch were not all his either. He had no share in game, either snared or shot in the nearby forest. Few peasants had more than one cow and a few fowls. In the country they lived on a thin porridge, vegetable broth, onions, turnips, cabbage, garlic, and rye bread. On Sundays and great feasts, the woman of the house might be able to please the family with a flat rye pasty stuffed with mushrooms. Otherwise, her children would creep to the edge of the neighboring forest, lift their shirts, and fill them with berries. If a peasant kept bees, he might be lucky to have a small crock of honey for his use.

The bigger villages had inns and sold kvass, honey mead, and local beer, all equally potent. These inns were not frequented by the gentry but by the small merchants and by peasants. The latter had no money, but payment in kind was accepted, and innkeepers wisely asked no questions about the provenance of a hare or a woodcock. Poaching carried grim penalties, and a Muscovite peasant was shrewd enough not to be caught with a pike or a hare under his arm.

The Muscovite peasants faced three main perils: a long drought, which meant a poor harvest, when the women would have to churn unripe grain and even stubble into something remotely resembling flour; various ailments of the flesh, which had no cure

other than oddly colored herb cordials; and, finally,
the constant fear of the tax collectors. These officials,
themselves shockingly underpaid, made ends meet by
graft. A peasant usually had to add an extra half sack
of grain "to sweeten" the tax collector.

Peasants were baptized, married, and buried according to the Orthodox rites, but the village churches had
none of the splendid and moving ceremonial carried
out in great monasteries and city cathedrals. The village clergy, themselves of peasant stock, were ignorant
and knew just enough to mumble through their office

books. Peasants attended Mass and Vespers in spring and summer, but there was no sermon at either service. The mere idea of a priest "preaching the Gospel" would have bewildered the congregation, whose piety consisted of frequent signs of the cross, prostrations, kissing what few ikons there were, and lighting what thin tallow candles they could afford. Parish priests demanded their due for any service performed, a due necessarily in kind—mushrooms, kindling, root vegetables, peas, eggs. Such payments, together with the yield of their own patch of land, were the clergy's means of livelihood.

There was no education as we understand it. Few indeed were the peasants who knew the Lord's Prayer. They had a vague idea about the Trinity, but the idea varied from district to district. In a village not far from Tver the Trinity meant Christ, the Virgin, and St. Nicholas. A drop of oil, blessed by the priest, was believed to possess magical powers. But processions, led by a priest up and down a drought-stricken field, never ended the drought.

Superstitions, inherited from the remote pagan past, continued to thrive most vigorously There was hardly a village without its *znakhar* or *znakharka*, a knowing man or woman, versed in witchcraft. They dealt in roots, herbs, and obscure incantations. They could put the evil eye on humankind and on animals. Moonlight had a language for them; so had thunderstorms. They were called to help a woman in labor, and their assistance was asked for in a peasant's last hour. The authorities did not interfere. It seemed as though the "dark art" was part and parcel of a peasant's daily life, and his Christian allegiance was interwoven with pre-Christian beliefs. An elm, uprooted by a storm, meant death. A good crop of wild raspberries promised a happy month.

Yet, hard and penurious as their life was, it ran on natural runnels. Birth brought no joy and death no grief. Another child meant an extra mouth to feed. A peasant's death was the inevitable end to all the ceaseless frets of life.

There were neither courts nor lawyers in those days. A man with a grievance applied to the nearest landowner for redress. The landowner listened to the plaintiff and the defendant and sent them off to the next town for "justice." This was brutally simple: the two men would be ordered to fight and whoever won was declared to be innocent, the circumstances of the grievance wholly disregarded, and some such fights ended fatally for the innocent defendant. A first theft, once discovered and proved, meant a flogging; the second, a mutilation; and a third trespass led to the gallows. Brigands, once caught, were hanged without a trial, and murderers suffered the same penalty. Any merchant had the right to dispose of his property if he had sons, but no daughters could inherit, and if the man had no male heirs in the family, his entire substance went to the treasury in Moscow. Every provincial town had a prison for tax defaulters and others accused of nonviolent crimes. The prison was called *yama*, or "hole." It was built underground and had neither light nor heat. Men were sent there at the local bigwig's pleasure; they had no trial and did not know the length of their sentence. They were kept alive by charity: monks and local merchants brought food and water. The *yama* officials did not consider it necessary to feed the prisoners.

Chapter V

In 1546 Muscovy stood at the threshold of momentous changes. Ivan's coming of age was marked by more than the peals from all the capital's belfries. At the session of the Duma he told the hierarchy and nobility that he had decided to be a czar. The very next year he chose Anastasia Romanova for his czarina, and he could not have made a happier choice. Anastasia came from an old, untitled family who were not of Rurik descent and kept aloof from factions. The young Czarina "showered gold and silver with one look of her eyes," and from the beginning she influenced her young husband with her gentleness, her common sense, her compassion for all the hard-driven folk of Muscovy. Many men there were who had cause to fear the Czar's displeasure, but few of them failed to find a successful mediator in Anastasia, who possessed the rare ability to convince a stubborn mind that mercy counted for more than anger. Though she agreed with Ivan that the boyars' arrogant autocracy must be checked, she pleaded for the lessening of taxes and for more humane treatment of those kept in jails. Finally, Anastasia reminded Ivan of his early teens, his affection for the humble folk, and their trust in him.

Sylvester, a priest, and Adashev, a layman of lowly birth and high promise, became the young Czar's counselors.

In the same year of 1546, at an open-air meeting in Moscow, Ivan made a remarkable speech to a vast crowd of commoners. He told them that he meant to draw closer to his people and to lighten their burdens. The nobility thought him mad, conscious as they were that the day of their power was over. Copies of the speech were sent all over Muscovy and read to all the illiterate folk. It seemed like a May dawn for the country.

Ivan had hated the aristocracy since his childhood and an autocrat's hatred in Muscovy would have led to numerous executions. It was Anastasia's influence which made the first Czar turn toward the path of peaceful reform. The boyars still lived in splendor; their fabulous wealth was not confiscated and they still sat in the Duma. But the Czar was guided by the counsels of "simple men" like Adashev and others who, well acquainted with national problems, knew how to deal with them. The first Czar and his wife won the affection of the poorest plowman.

Anastasia was for peace at home, but Ivan's predecessors had had to fight many wars, and the Czarina wisely abstained from influencing matters of foreign policy. Muscovy's growing wealth increased the enmity of her neighbors—Sweden, Livonia, Lithuania, Poland, as well as the Khan of Kazan, whose power stretched all over the lower reaches of the Volga and reached Astrakhan. This area was a huge but difficult terrain of forests, marshes, and deep lakes; Ivan saw that its conquest would mean the final blow to the Tartar invaders and the possession of the Caspian Sea with its rich fisheries.

Muscovy's military strength consisted of over three hundred thousand men, but more than half of them had to guard the western boundaries, and Ivan would not recruit anyone engaged in trade and husbandry.

Having sent a challenge to the Khan of Kazan, Ivan left his Czarina to her works of benevolence and moved out of Moscow in the spring of 1552 at the head of 150,000 men, who heard their Czar singing lustily: "Lord, we are moving in Thy name." Anastasia had already given him two daughters and was pregnant again, and the Czar's prayers were rather divided between the happy issue of the campaign and the birth of an heir.

The Khan thought Kazan was impregnable. He also hoped the Turks would come to his help if he was attacked. By the autumn of 1552, however, both Kazan and Astrakhan were in Muscovite hands, and the scattered remnants of the Tartar host had disappeared, rushing south to the Crimea. "The Czar's hand lay over the Caspian." The Muscovite victory left the Western enemies aghast, and Sweden and Livonia quickly decided on a peace treaty with their powerful neighbor.

The Czar turned back to the north. At no great distance from Moscow, a mud-bespattered messenger brought news to the Czar's tent: Anastasia had given birth to a son. Ivan wept for joy.

Back in his capital, reunited with his wife, enraptured with his tiny son—who was christened Dimitry in honor of Prince Dimitry Donskoy of Moscow, the first man to challenge the Tartars—Ivan felt triumphant indeed. The signing of the peace treaties increased his happiness. He had the merchantry of Moscow summoned to the Kremlin and told them that they could trade "without let or hindrance" in Sweden, Lübeck, Antwerp, England, France, and Spain, and he assured the merchants that "ships would be there to carry their cargoes."

That was a hope hard to realize. Muscovy had no harbors; the Baltic was closed to her; the Caspian Sea was really a locked-in lake.

There was another disappointment. The first campaign led by Ivan had revealed innumerable technical deficiencies. Muscovite artillery was virtually nonexistent and the country had no experienced sappers. The Czar needed foreign gunners, armorers, and other skilled artisans to instruct and develop the nation's talent. The ambassadors' *prikaz*, or council, in Moscow was told to draft letters from Ivan to all the friendly foreign countries. He explained his need and set out most advantageous terms for men willing to enter his service.

But the Emperor Charles V, whose writ ran all over Europe—with the exception of England—disliked and feared any possibility of Muscovy's advance. He looked upon the Muscovites as boors, if not barbarians. He heard of the Kazan victory and decided that no Flemish, Dutch, or German "man of skill" was to go to Muscovy.

In Moscow the Emperor's harsh *diktat* was treated with contempt. The imperial ambassadors were received in audience as politely as befitted their rank, but there was a sense of distance and the gentlemen were not invited to break bread at the Czar's table.

Yet Ivan was not discomfited. Charles V's open unfriendliness gave a sharper edge to the Czar's resolve to win harbors for Muscovy. Denmark, as he knew well, took slight notice of imperial decisions, but for the Muscovite ships to reach Denmark meant running the gauntlet of many dangers in the Baltic waters. So Ivan told Adashev, his chief adviser, that the Baltic must be drawn into the Muscovite net.

Ivan focused his attention on Livonia, for he saw the opportunity of winning at least a foothold near the coveted Baltic shore. This time Ivan stayed in Moscow while his army moved westward in the spring of 1553. So successful were the Muscovites that early in 1554 Livonia pleaded for a truce. The Czar granted it on his own terms and these were harsh. A few years later, what few foreigners there were in Ivan's service began building a harbor near the Narva estuary. Livonia stirred uneasily; the truce was broken and the ensuing war went against them. The town of Narva was taken in 1558. "Now," said the Czar, "our trade can expand."

Chapter VI

Trade in Moscow came in for a busy time. On occasions imports exceeded exports, but imports were so highly taxed that the treasury amassed enormous profits. A single bolt of Flemish cloth brought a return five times greater than ten bales of Muscovite homespun. Novgorod, still clinging to a semblance of its civic independence despite all the ravages dealt it by Ivan III, remained the greatest market. The Novgorod merchants knew the routes by water and overland: they had learned many tricks of the trade from the foreigners within their gates. They continued exporting flax, hemp, undressed hides, honey, and wax, and their fine pottery had begun attracting the attention of Scandinavian countries. Novgorod had also learned the art of dressing and coloring leather. In Moscow, the court and nobility wore soft yellow, red, and green boots made by Novgorod cobblers. The Novgorod shops remained a cynosure for Muscovite ladies. There were glassworks which turned out exquisite goblets, bowls, and necklaces in clear white, pale green, and blue. Nor did Novgorod forget the children. There were toy shops with dolls and animals molded of clay or cunningly carved of wood, and painted most realistically. A crate of tiny wolves, bears, polecats, fowls, and swans reached the Kremlin for the amusement of the infant Prince Dimitry.

In the sixteenth century Muscovy had no sugar, but the people had early learned how to use honey. Tula and Viazma produced exquisite gingerbread, which was not scorned at the table of Swedish kings. Kholmogory in the north supplied rare furs, greatly valued in the West, particularly ermine and sable. Its great salt mines, however primitively worked, yielded much for home consumption, as did the salt mines of Stararussa. Farther south, Yaroslav and its neighborhood brought incredible yields of grain—wheat, rye, barley, oats, buckwheat, and millet known as *psheno*. In those provinces, rye alone was sown in late autumn. The rest of the cereals went in at the beginning of the spring.

But by far the greatest wealth of Muscovy came from fish. With the acquisition of the Caspian Sea, the industry took a great leap forward. The Muscovites soon learned that caviar, the soft roe of *bieluga, sveruga,* and *sterliad,* three fishes unknown outside these waters, was prized in the West for its delicacy. Caviar became more or less a state monopoly; subjected to heavy dues, it was exported in tubs duly sealed with official leaden seals. The market for fish in the West had necessarily dwindled since the Reformation, when the medieval Church fasts and abstinences were no longer observed in Protestant countries, but Muscovy still needed most of her fish for home consumption. The Orthodox Church had many more fasts than the Western Church; their observances were not so much custom as law, and a housewife, whatever her social rank, risked the accusation of heresy if she dared to serve, for example, a dish of roasted eggs on Christmas Eve.

Furs and timber headed the lists of valuable exports. By that time the Muscovites had become skilled furriers. Properly treated, skins of sable, ermine, mink, fox, wolf, and bear brought high prices. No foreign *gost*, or trader, missed the great fur market in Moscow, and fur merchants' wealth was prodigious in spite of the high taxation.

Muscovite birch and oak were also in demand abroad, but during Ivan's reign there was little exporting of grain, as special permits were needed for this.

Ivan's domains were vast, and he was resolved to expand them. He suspected that the unknown land far to the east, beyond the grim Urals, would yield fabulous returns in mineral and iron ore. Indeed, before his reign was ended, that vast unknown land was to be christened Siberia and peopled by daring explorers from Muscovy, who risked much but gained more. The merchant family of the Strogonovs penetrated that region and held it for the Czar, and he granted them one concession after another.

It may appear that the grain permits, which were not issued freely, were an oblique measure of relief for this or that corner of Muscovy stricken by famine. But, in fact, their immediate purpose was to produce a tax from the grain and seed merchants. Trade certainly expanded, but the Czar's expansionist policy increased military expenditure. Taxes and tolls grew in proportion. Even a countrywoman, taking her pumpkins, mushrooms, and whortleberries to the local market, would be taxed on her modest proceeds.

Social life in Moscow and elsewhere presented a curious phenomenon. The court and the higher ranks still religiously observed the law of the *terem*, and Czarina Anastasia kept it most faithfully. The first lady in the land was never seen at her husband's banquets or in his audience room.

The menfolk among the nobility had far wider social horizons. They gave prodigious banquets at their mansions and attended festivities outside. They ate much and drank more. In autumn and winter they rode out hunting the boar, bear, and wolf. In summer they had gay falconry parties, or fished on the banks of the Moskva and the Yauza, or broke fresh horses outside the gates of Moscow. Some of them attended the Duma. All were present in the audience hall at audiences given to foreign ambassadors. Later, some among them were invited to the Czar's table.

Social life was wholly different among the lower

ranks, though some wealthy merchants kept their
womenfolk in rigid seclusion. The "ordinary folk"
had no space for a *terem* in their small wooden houses.
Among them a family was a closely knit unit, the
housewife and her daughters breaking bread together
with the husband and grownup sons. From such houses
the wife, attended by a maidservant, went to the markets and bargained for a piece of bacon, a hare, or a
sack of apples. And at the markets she listened and
learned about the latest victory or defeat of the Czar's
armies, about a famine near Vologda, a flame-tailed
comet seen over Tver, and a higher tax put on honey

mead and on poultry. There were two printing presses in Moscow, but no news sheets and no schools. Very few, if any, women knew their letters.

Far wider social liberties were enjoyed in the heart of the country. Men and women, boys and girls shared the day's hard work and enjoyed what leisure fell to them, no artificial barriers hampering them. In the lush golden summer days, the working stint done, the village folk would meet, sing, and dance barefoot on the silken grass. The married women's hair hid by a kerchief, the girls' plaits tumbling down to their waists, they danced with the innate grace of born dancers, blissfully unaware that they were shaping a great inheritance for centuries to come. They danced to no other accompaniment but the clapping of the men's hands and the unconscious sense of rhythm within themselves. When dusk fell, modest refreshments were offered—kvass, a pasty of onions and mushrooms, a trug of berries.

On two or three occasions in the summer there were fairs in bigger villages and towns. The people trudged barefoot, a satchel of food over the shoulder, a few coppers carefully tied into a corner of a kerchief. They might buy a hair ribbon, an earthenware pot, a handful of seed, but, more than anything else, they knew they would enjoy themselves. There was always a red and blue painted merry-go-round, much singing and dancing, rough but welcome fare, and garlands of poppies, cornflowers, and other wild blossoms from the nearest wood. For children there were straw dolls, their faces accurately marked with a stick of charred wood; there were strings of cheap, gaily colored beads for girls and wooden whistles for boys. A tent served for a *kabák*, and men got drunk, but not before they had bought some tokens for their families. The merry-making went on into the small hours, and voices kept on singing songs in praise of a czar whom few among them had seen, and of a czarina they were never likely to see.

Chapter VII

Czarina Anastasia was barely sixteen when she married Ivan in 1547. She bore him six children: three daughters who died in infancy and three sons. The eldest son, Dimitry, died of a fever in 1553. Anastasia had two more boys, Ivan and Fedor. In 1560, not yet thirty, she succumbed to a fever no physician could cure, and died.

Her death felled Ivan. For thirteen years she had been a loved wife and a wise counselor. She had brought out the best in him. She had guided him toward the paths of clemency and justice. She had fanned his affection and respect for the "poor people." In brief, had Anastasia not died in 1560, Ivan IV, the first Czar of Muscovy, might never have been known in history as Ivan the Terrible.

When his wife's funeral rites were over, the Czar left the capital and shut himself up in a neighboring abbey. Received with customary honors, he told the abbot that he wanted a cell to be alone in. He did not appear at any services and he barely touched the food that was brought him. Just thirty, he had the appearance of an aged man. All light had gone out of his eyes; his hands trembled, his cheeks were sunken, his lips seemed locked in. On rare occasions he would summon the abbot, tell him that with Anastasia's death everything was over, that he, the Czar, wished to abdicate and assume a monk's habit, that his son, Ivan the Younger, should ascend the throne. The abbot, a simple-minded man, had nothing but platitudes to offer his guest. The late Czarina was in paradise; he, the Czar, should not grieve so much, everything happened according to God's will. But the truisms fell on deaf ears. Ivan sat motionless, no expression on his face. It was Anastasia he wanted and not the pious prattle of a monk.

Meanwhile, Moscow was in turmoil. From one end of the city to the other, rumors flew that the beloved Czarina had been poisoned, and two unfortunate artisans were drowned in the Yauza for having repeated the rumor in public. At the Kremlin, nurses looked after the two little Princes, who, understanding nothing and afraid of everything, cried for their parents' return.

The loss of Anastasia had indeed killed the best in the Czar. He came back to the Kremlin, his heart hardened, his manner rough toward the household. He read reports, dictated letters, announced various decisions, yet his face was like an iron mask, and none could read his mind. Outwardly, Ivan's grip on the nation's affairs was as firm as ever. He watched military preparations for the coming campaign against Poland and Sweden, and studied the Turkish danger, the Sultan having become suspiciously friendly with the remnants of the Kazan Tartars now sheltered on the borders of the Crimea.

Before that year was over, Moscow was buzzing with the latest news: the priest Sylvester, and Adashev, the Czar's advisers, accused by an unknown person of having poisoned Anastasia, had been removed from the Kremlin. The Czar did not order their execution: these two closest and most loyal friends were sent into lifelong exile in the remote reaches of Muscovy. The nobility said that now the Czar must have new councilors. His commanders, Prince Andrey Kurbsky, Prince Serebrianin, and others, loyal to a man, were about to leave the capital. During the farewell audience, following a solemn Te Deum for victory, the Czar wished them success and spoke so benevolently that the men left in good spirits.

Nobody knew that the dismissal of Sylvester and Adashev was but a prelude to more than twenty years of unspeakable horrors and that the Czar was haunted by the idea that treason surrounded him. Treason, he felt convinced, would come from the old aristocracy. What could be easier for his enemies than to have him and his two sons poisoned? Knowing that the cream of his army, the *strielzy*, or sharpshooters, recruited

from the masses, were loyal to him, Ivan ordered two
companies to remain behind and guard the Kremlin
Palace. All food and drink served to Ivan and his sons
had first to be tasted by gentlemen of the household.

These orders and many others like them were outward expressions of a mind grown deeply suspicious.
Ivan's earliest memories were taking on clearer shape
and color. Then he had been a child. Now that he was
a grown man, his hatred of the ancient nobility, the
same hatred once calmed and checked by Anastasia's
influence, was swelling most alarmingly. It pleased
him to notice that those proud men were afraid of his

step, voice, and glance. But Ivan did not hurry with his terrible plans.

Accompanied by a picked bodyguard, Ivan would still often ride into the countryside. Once there, suspicion and hatred fell from his shoulders. Among the peasantry and the poorer town folk, the Czar breathed freely. Those people, he said to himself, would still be loyal and affectionate. From their ranks he would choose a very special trained unit to carry out his orders for what Ivan called the cleansing from Muscovy of the aristocratic rot.

Had the Czar indeed chosen such men, history might not have known him as the Terrible.

But he did not. Unfortunately, the men who began to follow him were self-seeking men ready to serve him because, by placing them above the law, Ivan absolved them from any crime committed for his supposed safety. The unit was called *oprichnyki* (defenders). Soon the word became synonymous with cruelty surpassing that of the Tartars. The two most infamous men in that crowd of hangmen, torturers, and cutthroats were Basmanov and Skuratin. Few in the unit had any morality. They came from the lowest dregs of society, summoned to serve as *oprichnyki* because of their blood lust. This dreadful new bodyguard of Ivan's had a jail, known as *zastiónok*, in the grounds of the Kremlin where innocent "suspects," boyars who had probably never plotted against the Czar or belonged to any factions, would be tortured to death.

It might appear that Ivan had gone mad. One by

one, many ancient families, their origins going back to the days of Rus, were destroyed. Not the head of the family only, but his wife, children, and kin perished. The terrified clergy of Moscow obediently sang requiems for their souls, and the Czar kept a special book in which he entered their names "for prayers in perpetuity." His vengeance flamed higher still when some noblemen succeeded in escaping from Muscovy. Among them was one of his most famous commanders, Prince Andrey Kurbsky, who escaped to Lithuania, then at war with Muscovy.

The Metropolitan of Moscow, Philip, was a man of matchless courage. He had the right of entry into the Czar's apartments and there he told him, in the name of all the Orthodox Christians in the land, to put an end to the executions. Philip urged the Czar to repent of all these enormities. He did not threaten God's vengeance but spoke gravely, a wooden cross held in his hands. The Czar wept, struck his breast, and vowed to amend. But Philip was doomed. Not long after, in his cell, while at prayer for the Czar, the most courageous Metropolitan of Muscovy was strangled by Skuratin.

Novgorod was cruelly sacked "for treason," thousands of the population butchered by the *oprichnyki*. Yet, strangely enough, the countryside remained quiet. The peasants were convinced that the Czar needed defenders from the noblemen plotting against his life. When in an outburst of wrath Ivan struck his son and heir, wielding his staff of silver and iron so hard that the youth fell dead, an incredible version of the crime was winged over Muscovy. The Czar had meant to chastise, not to kill. Otherwise, he would not have sobbed at his son's bier. As to the old nobility, argued the common folk, they had oppressed the poor for generations and now they had their deserts.

In the city, terror burned high, sank to embers, and flamed up again. During "peaceful" spells, the Czar accused himself of his crimes, in some abbey or other. When in Moscow, he attended all the services, his piety more fervent than ever. But the dreadful bodyguard was not dismissed.

Chapter VIII

Executioners were busy "uprooting treason" and grass grew in the spacious grounds of many a mansion, its former owners gone to the stake or the gibbet. The Moscow sun rose and set in blood. At the Kremlin Palace, the Czar's youngest son, now the heir, Prince Fedor, was growing up, gentle and delicate, his tutors' delight, his physicians' despair.

Muscovy trod a path ever widened by the Czar's ambition. The merchant clan of the Strogonovs crossed the Urals, and Eastern Siberia became part of Muscovy. But there were still the coveted Baltic harbors. Wars with Livonia and Sweden went on. Trade flourished and the Czar's government carried on its business. The army grew in numbers, its needs leaping higher and higher. So did taxation. Peasants murmured, merchants grumbled.

It was when Ivan was away in the west, trying to

loosen Livonia's hold on the Baltic, that he heard most disquieting news: Suleiman II, Sultan of Turkey, was threatening to capture Kazan. Tartar hordes, urged by Turkish counsels and helped by Turkish money, were moving north. The Czar veered eastward, but not in time. By 1571 the Tartars had breached the gates of Moscow, burning, pillaging, murdering. Not till the following year were they beaten off, never to trouble Muscovy again—but the damage done by them was enormous. Every timbered house outside the Kremlin walls was burned down.

It was about this time that Ivan, always eager for fresh blood and new faces, met a man in his early twenties. "He met him by chance," say the chroniclers, and no more. We cannot tell what that "chance" was. Of humble beginnings, from remote Tartar stock, but a very pious Orthodox Christian, Boris Godunov lived in Moscow with his sister Irina. According to tradition, Boris knew his letters and earned his livelihood as a clerk. Ivan was struck by his grasp of national affairs and soon Boris was an intimate at the palace. He had no definite post and he never joined the *oprichnyki*. But he became a necessity to the Czar.

Even the life Ivan had led since Anastasia's death, with drunken bouts and other excesses, could not cloud his mind. In Boris the Czar recognized someone capable of seizing and expanding his own ideas. Boris looked at the Western map with a visionary's eyes, but his suggestions about foreign policy were those of a shrewd statesman.

Meanwhile, in spite of continuing wars with Poland, Lithuania, Sweden, and Livonia, Muscovy had acquired a new friend—England.

The White Sea route, opened by Richard Chancellor, offered advantages to both countries. Under Edward VI and Mary Tudor, treaties were signed; the Czar's ambassadors voyaged to England and returned bringing engineers, "men skilled in all manner of weapons," shipwrights, mining experts, and physicians. Ivan welcomed them with open arms. A trading company was formed and showered with privileges no other alien had ever enjoyed in Muscovy. The English were exempt from all taxes and tolls.

Elizabeth Tudor proved herself a firm friend. The Polish and Livonian representatives in England saw great danger in the *rapprochement*. "The Muscovites are barbarians; often enough did we defeat them before, but now the Czar is building ships at Narva, with English shipwrights in his service. His army used to be little more than an ill-equipped, wild horde. Now the Czar has gunnery experts from England and much wise counsel. His successes have weakened Lithuania. He has his eyes on the Baltic; he might overrun Scandinavia and then turn south to the Low Countries, to France, to England. The Queen of England should not trust him."

But Elizabeth Tudor shrugged these warnings away. The Muscovite trade brought wealth to England. She asked for no more and continued writing friendly letters to Ivan. In 1567 the Czar offered the

Queen asylum in Muscovy if she ever needed it. He never proposed to Elizabeth, but toward the end of his life the Czar made inquiries about the Queen's cousin, Lady Mary Hastings. These preliminaries led to nothing.

Ivan's matrimonial ventures were many. Anastasia had given him six children, four of whom died in infancy. Between 1565 and 1582 the Czar married six times. One wife escaped to a convent and four died, setting off rumors of poison at the hands of the Czar's secret enemies. Yet nearly all Kremlin-fostered rumors were so many fables. Not one of these five wives had a child. The seventh and last wife, Maria Nagaya, bore a son, christened Dimitry; and she outlived her husband. Canonically, four of the seven alliances were invalid since no member of the Orthodox Church might marry more than three times. But the hierarchy dared not protest.

Meanwhile, the heir, Prince Fedor, came to his late teens and was married to the sister of his father's friend, Irina Godunova. Boris still held no official rank at court, but paid reverence to Ivan and Fedor as well as to his sister, now the future Czarina. Little Dimitry, Maria Nagaya's son, was still a baby living among women.

In houses all over Moscow and up and down the countryside, anxiety stalked. This time it was no idle rumor but a disturbing fact. The Czar's health was failing. Excesses could not cripple his vigorous mind, but they avenged themselves on his flesh. In April

1584, at the age of fifty-three, the first Czar of Muscovy died. The merchants, the townsfolk, and the peasants mourned him sincerely. The nobility thought they could breathe again.

For all its horrors and excesses, Ivan IV's was a remarkable reign. Trade kept finding new outlets, but trading induced more than buying and selling. There was an awakened thirst for culture, foreign habits, a curiosity to find out about foreign achievements. Though ancient usages were not uprooted, the cultural climate of Moscow became subtly different. Literacy increased. The huge volume of governmental business alone demanded clerks and secretaries able to read and write. Even merchants no longer cut notches in their tallies. The sovereign being an educated man, it became fashionable to master Latin and German and to gain some acquaintance of maps so that Spain no longer seemed the end of the world. Strides in architecture, painting, and mosaics were made, and native handicrafts began to be appreciated.

Above all else, there were suggestions of tremendous social changes. High rank no longer automatically opened the doors to advancement. Apart from the *oprichnyki*, the common folk were given an opportunity to serve Muscovy in more mentally rewarding ways than plowing a furrow or counting turnips at a market stall. Obscurity of origin ceased to be an obstacle. Boris Godunov offers an outstanding example of this changing attitude.

Chapter IX

Irina Godunova, now Czarina of Muscovy, watched her husband's coronation through a latticed window. The same day in June 1584 her brother, Boris, was publicly proclaimed chief Councilor of State, and Elizabeth Tudor addressed letters to him as well as to the young Czar. At the very next sitting of the Duma, Boris had his chair just one step below and to the right of Fedor's throne, the Czar being his closest friend, brother-in-law, and sovereign, in that order. It then seemed that there were no more heights for Boris to climb.

Pious, gentle, delicate from birth, deeply in love with his wife, and most happily at his ease with Boris, Czar Fedor was twenty-five. One cloud, however, remained on the horizon: he had no children.

Ivan IV's will was solemnly read out and its provisions honored faithfully. He left a large and wealthy

patrimony to his infant son, Prince Dimitry, and
made it a condition that his widow, Maria Nagaya,
was not to lack either necessities or luxuries. The
Dowager Czarina left for Uglich with her baby son,
her women, and an immense crowd of household servants and others. Normally, the Dowager could have
remained in the Kremlin *terem*, but its mistress was
now Irina, and Ivan's seventh wife preferred independence and the freedom of choosing her own dinner.

In Moscow, Boris stood at the helm of the state—
always in the name of the Czar. Fedor was by no
means limited, but his constant ill health banned the
least exertion. The favorite Muscovite diversions—

fishing, falconry, hunting the bear, wolf, and boar—
were beyond his strength. He shirked no duties; he sat
in the Duma, gave formal audiences, listened to what
documents Boris read to him, and signed them. Otherwise, his time was spent in devotions, games of chess,
reading, and talking to his Czarina. Food meant nothing to the young Czar. He avoided banquets and, according to ancient custom, dined alone, but most of
the ceremonially served dishes were carried out untouched. Milk, gruel, a little boiled fish, and an apple
—Fedor asked for no more. Apart from duties of piety,
his true refreshment came in his wife's company. Irina
soothed and comforted him, and assured him that, under her brother's guidance, all would go well with the
country, and Irina neither flattered nor exaggerated.

All was, indeed, going well with Muscovy. From
the start of the new reign there was a policy of con-
ciliation. The army could have breasted any campaign and the treasury borne any expenditure, but
peace, according to Boris, was of far greater advantage.
The commonalty, peasants in particular, benefited
immediately from lightened taxation. The huge profits
stemming from the newly discovered Siberian wealth
were used for the betterment of countryside conditions. Roads were improved. A police corps, known
as *pristavy* and recruited from among the reliable
countrymen, kept brigands and vagabonds in check.
The peasants' tithes, paid in kind, were reduced and
the most humble rural household could now enjoy
some variety in their monotonous diet. The country
clergy were reminded that God had mercy on all shorn

sheep, and were no longer allowed to take the last fowl from a peasant's widow in payment for her husband's funeral. Whenever the peasants heard Boris's name, they crossed themselves and blessed him.

In Moscow, the boyar Duma was at first difficult. In the end its members had to admit that the "Tartar upstart" could govern. He had no equal in his grip on foreign affairs. His adroit diplomacy quieted the Khan of the Crimea and the Sultan of Turkey. He succeeded in establishing peace on the western borders of Muscovy. He proved to Sweden that "peace is far more profitable than war," and Stockholm grew quiet.

Little by little, Boris was accepted by all social ranks in Muscovy. An undeniable upstart, his origins obscure, he succeeded in winning popularity among all. Boris married well, and had a son and a daughter.

In 1591 a thunderbolt crashed over Moscow when messengers, smothered in dust from head to foot, galloped through the Kremlin gates. Prince Dimitry, the Czar's half brother and heir, aged about nine, had died at Uglich. "A mischance," said the official report. The boy, known to suffer from epileptic fits, had fallen on a knife. But the people of Uglich chose to believe differently. Like a tongue of flame over stubble in the field, the story ran throughout Muscovy: "murder" and "murder" again until jealousy against the "Tartar upstart" turned to venom. Broadsheets, printed by unknown men, appeared in towns and villages. Some rural clergy, themselves confused, read them to peasants, and suspicion would have become conviction if Boris had not acted promptly. A commission of inquiry was dispatched to Uglich with Prince Vassily Shuyskie at the head. It was conclusively proved that the little Prince had fatally hurt himself while in an epileptic fit. The commission discovered instances of inadequate supervision and those responsible were punished. Little by little, the turmoil died down.

Yet the problem remained: Czar Fedor was the last of his line. The hierarchy and others tried to win his consent to a measure that would hardly have been popular in Muscovy, where people loved the Czarina. Fedor was asked to put Irina into a convent and marry another girl, who would bear him an heir. The gentle Czar refused firmly and angrily.

About 1596, Czar Fedor's health took a turn for the worse. One by one, boyar factions were formed, and some noblemen left for their manors, where discussions were safer held than in the capital.

Early in 1598, Fedor died. By law and custom he could have named a successor, since there were many men of Rurik descent to start another dynasty. But Fedor had not done this. The house which had ruled over Rus and Muscovy for 736 years had come to an end. The land had no sovereign and the Muscovite habit of plunging into grim prophecies came well to the fore. It looked as though the great country was on the brink of civil war. Over the western border and in the south, Muscovy's enemies began getting ready for an invasion. Even the enfeebled Lithuania hoped for her share of the booty, and the Crimean Tartars were certain of seeing the crescent rise again over Kazan and Astrakhan.

Chapter X

The commonalty, most of them illiterate, still hoped that their *laskovye*, or kindly man, Boris, would remain at the helm. But there was unrest, caused by the Czar's death and the inevitable rumors. Wild-eyed, tattered soothsayers tramped from one village to another, asserting that the end of the world was near, shouting that Czar Fedor, like Elijah of old, had been bodily taken into the heavens and still watched over the country. A superstitious frenzy took hold of the peasants, who stayed surprisingly sober and as surprisingly idle. The sowing time went by, while they waited idly for something to reassure them.

Boris was still in Moscow. The boyar factions, as he knew too well, were planning his downfall, but the merchantry, the common citizens of the capital, and, above all, the military were on his side. Unfortunately, at that moment a number of regiments had to be sent

to Smolensk to ward off a Polish attack, and to Pskov, threatened by Sweden.

It was left to the Duma to elect a successor to Fedor. Name after name was called out and failed to win a majority. Then the people of the old city rose as one man: they wanted Boris for Czar. Metropolitan Iona counseled the Duma to accept the people's decision. The nobility, afraid of the mob's anger, gave in.

But the popularly elected "upstart" could not be found at the Kremlin Palace. His sister, the Dowager Czarina Irina, had gone into a convent after the Czar's funeral, and Boris had left the Kremlin to be with his sister. It was a time of worry for Irina: in spite of the difference in age between them, she knew her brother well. She guessed that not only the capital but the whole country wanted him for its sovereign, and she knew this would answer his own ambition; she knew equally well that he might refuse the crown.

But Boris did not confide in her. Somber-eyed and silent, his beard tangled, he spent whole days in an outer cell of the abbey, barely touching his food and seeing nobody except a clerk and a servant. It was some time before Moscow found him at the abbey. Deputation after deputation rode over to ask him to accept the crown, and Boris kept refusing it. In the end, a crowd of commoners rushed to the gates, stormed their way in, knelt, wept, and implored their "father and benefactor" to rule over them. Still grieving for her husband, Irina joined her pleas to theirs. "For God's sake and Muscovy's," she begged, and Boris gave in.

Late in the spring of 1598 he was crowned, the first and last man of obscure origins to be raised to the Muscovite throne.

His finely developed sense of statesmanship was as keen as ever. So was his inbred shrewdness. He knew he could count on the military, the merchantry, and the commonalty. But the nobility, for all their oaths of allegiance, stayed aloof. For the first time in his life Boris was gripped by the iron clutch of insecurity. Inevitably, insecurity led to mistakes.

Always eager to strengthen the links with the West, Boris included all foreign imports when announcing the lessening of duties. To offset the losses to the treasury, he raised the export tolls, to the displeasure of Muscovite merchants. Higher taxation meant a rise in prices in the home markets, and the commonalty took to murmuring. Complaints thickened when Muscovy learned that the Czar was about to betroth his only daughter, Xenia, to Prince Johan of Denmark.

In the Muscovite mind the mere idea of an Orthodox girl marrying a foreigner and a heretic—and that girl the Czar's daughter—suggested an alliance with sulphur and brimstone. The unlucky Prince came to Moscow to fetch his bride and succumbed to a fatal fever before the wedding day, the populace interpreting his death as a sign of God's anger. Little by little, from one town to another, Boris's popularity began to wane.

In token of his piety he raised the Metropolitan of Moscow to the rank of Patriarch, but the measure pleased neither the hierarchy nor the laity. "What is a patriarch?" the commonalty asked, bewildered by a word they had never heard before. "Does the Czar wish to set a Latin Pope over us?" murmured the nobility.

The latter, as Boris knew, were against him to a man. And here he committed his worst blunder. In his fear he exiled many members of the nobility to their manors south and west of Moscow, where they had ample opportunities to consort with Lithuania and Poland, the twin immemorial enemies of Muscovy.

And Boris knew little of manorial households. It never occurred to him that the numerous men there employed were in close touch with neighboring villages, their occupants always greedy for rumor and gossip. "The prince our master," would say a stableman, "has been exiled from Moscow—and why? The Czar has no use for Muscovites. He is all for foreigners. He would sell the whole country to them if they paid him enough. Why, in Moscow, my wife had to pay double the price for a tallow candle—all because of taxes. I have seen wealthy merchants' sons begging for bread."

Peasants listened avidly. The natural consequence of their fragmented understanding came out in spurts of violence here and there. They did not care a jot about the exiled noblemen cushioned in luxury in their manors. They did care about the additional burdens placed on their shoulders. Boris had once been adored by the commonalty, but such a popularity is feather-light. And when, in Moscow, the Czar heard of these occasional uprisings, his reaction was swift and unjust.

He announced measures to check the shortage of agricultural labor. He made it a legal offense for peasants to leave their villages and to change their employers; this measure marked the beginning of serfdom in Muscovy. Boris increased taxes and widened the powers of tax collectors, thus turning thousands upon thousands of friends into enemies. "Pray for the Czar?" a peasant would mutter at an inn. "I would rather pray for the devil."

In less than two years, his popularity became a sad memory. Numbers of young men sent by Boris to study commerce in Germany and the Low Countries were supposed to return by the end of 1602. Alarming reports of the Muscovite climate having reached them, they stayed on abroad and accepted service with foreign merchants. The young men argued that life under an alien sky was better than a possible mischance in their own country. The military alone remained loyal; Boris could rely on their support for his hunt for conspiracies both real and imagined, and his deepening sense of insecurity conjured up one phantom after another.

By law he had the right to name his successor. He willed the crown to his son Fedor and devoted much time to teaching him the craft of statesmanship. But Boris could not escape the thought that Fedor might never succeed him.

Ripple by ripple, the so-called *Smoútnoe Vremía*, the "Troubled Time," began spreading, and urban and rural circles became caught up in it, to say nothing of the capital.

Boris's spies were not idle. "Treason" became a commonplace word. At times, it looked as though the days of Ivan the Terrible were about to return. Reports of conspiracies reached the Czar daily. One of them pointed to the Romanov family, closely connected by marriage with the old Rurik dynasty and much favored by the late Czar Fedor, whose mother belonged to that clan.

Its head at the time was one Fedor, married, with one small son, Michael. The family was not executed. Instead, Fedor was sent to a remote monastery and forcibly turned into a monk, under the name of Philaret. His wife shared her husband's fate and disappeared into a nunnery, whose name was kept a secret. Their little son, then barely three years old, was sent to join his mother, the only comfort she had in her grief. One "nest of vipers" was rooted out of Moscow.

The Dowager Czarina, Maria Nagaya, last wife to Ivan the Terrible, now lived in a convent in the capital —a rather odd nun who bored the community with endless repetitions of all her misfortunes, too unimportant for her gossip to influence anyone. She never left the cloister.

Chapter XI

Sometime in 1602, messengers from the western
borders came to the Kremlin. They had been
pledged to secrecy, but the ride had been weary
and long and they had spent nights here and there,
sometimes growing garrulous in their cups. What they
had to tell reacted like a bomb on their listeners. Vast
reaches of Muscovy heard of the story before it reached
the Czar.

A youth in his early twenties who had been be-
friended by a Lithuanian nobleman had announced
that he was Dimitry, the youngest son of Ivan the
Terrible and the rightful sovereign of Muscovy. His
death at Uglich in 1591 had been a fable circulated
by the "Tartar upstart and usurper." The messengers
had been able to discover the Lithuanian's name: he
was the very wealthy Prince Mnishek and his young
guest was to be betrothed to the beautiful Marina
Mnishek.

The bombshell fell at the very time that the aftermath of a disastrous famine lay across great reaches of the country. Thousands of dispossessed, desperate men and women wandered about, marauding and killing for the sake of food. Soothsayers lost no time in shouting wherever they went that the famine, a comet seen earlier, and various other portents were so many proofs of God's displeasure with the present Czar.

Boris heard about the mysterious young man in Lithuania and dismissed the news as nonsense. The Czar's hands were full with the troubles at home. He forbade all speculation in grain and cereals; he abolished all taxes in the stricken areas, sent vast cartloads of food there, most of it bought at his own expense, ordered his provincial representatives to set up special tents where bread, turnips, bacon, meat, and fish were distributed free. Day and night he pored over the reports from the stricken regions and he dispatched what foreign physicians there were in Moscow to help the sick. Seeds, clothing, and kindling were needed, and Boris all but emptied his private treasury in his efforts to ease the sufferings of the people. He ordered the provincial governors and other officials to take no punitive measures against any victims of the famine accused of pillage or worse. He issued one proclamation after another to assure the people that he, their Czar, was ready to share his last crust with them. All the measures breathed a spirit of compassion, affection, and a burning readiness to help.

But the townsfolk and the peasants had lost their

affection and trust. They ate Boris's bread and porridge. They received many other tokens of his bounty. They muttered thanks, but their stormy hearts felt no gratitude. It was Boris Godunov's finest hour. Yet the commonalty remembered the hardships and forgot all else. Here and there, flickers of mutiny broke out. The authorities, ordered by the Czar to desist from punishment, found themselves blocked by one perplexity after another.

In early autumn of 1603 the mysterious young man left Lithuania and made for the south of Muscovy. Poles, Lithuanians, and Cossacks accompanied him. He rode ahead of that curious army, the ancient Rurik banner borne before him, and all his followers acknowledged his claim to be Ivan IV's son.

Boris ordered all his commanders present in Moscow to ride and crush the Pretender when the latter veered northward. Every city along the way greeted him with rapturous shouts: "Long live our rightful liege! Long live Czar Dimitry!" Yet Boris's spies reported that the shouts were not unanimous and that many people had stayed behind barred and bolted doors though crowds of peasants left their huts and joined the oddly assorted army, with axes and hatchets as their only weapons. Peasantry knew nothing about maneuvers and battles, but excitement urged them on.

In the end, the Muscovite army met the Pretender's host outside Sevsk and routed it completely. That first victory might have steered Muscovy into a saner, more tranquil course, but Boris's commanders wasted the

victory in a series of quarrels among themselves, and the Pretender seized on the chance this offered him. In the spring of 1605 he struck again. The odds would have been against him if many Muscovite troops had not decided to acknowledge him. The remnants of Boris's army were forced to flee north and south, east and west to escape the Kremlin wrath and the Pretender's vengeance. The way to Moscow lay open with no one to defend it.

On an April day in 1605 Boris, having finished his dinner, heard the appalling news and fell down in a seizure. There is no record of the details, though it is possible that he was poisoned.

Moscow rejoiced. Prince Vassily Shuyskie was compelled to stand on a dais in the Red Square in the Kremlin and confess to the crowds that he was a perjurer. "Listen, all you Christian people, Godunov meant Czar Ivan's little son to be murdered but the boy was rescued in time, and some other lad was killed instead. Long live Czar Dimitry!" The crowds cheered and clapped: they heard what they had wanted to hear.

Boris was not buried with the honors due to a czar. The very next day his widow, son, and daughter were strangled. Moscow had had enough of the Godunov stock. Even the military broke their allegiance. All the undeniable good done by Boris slipped out of the nation's memory. They held him guilty of having shed innocent blood in order to pave his way to a throne he had no right to occupy. Slander and rumor are hard to kill, and they permeated the national life for more than two centuries. At the time, nobody took the trouble to remember that Ivan IV's youngest son, subject to frequent epileptic fits, would scarcely have reached his teens.

The Godunov family having been wiped out, there followed a session of the Duma. It ended in a unanimous decision: the Pretender was to be acknowledged as the lawful sovereign of Muscovy.

The decision tore the country asunder. The dreadful *Smúta* (civil war) was no longer a distant phantom. It had turned into a reality, gripping Muscovy from end to end. With a few exceptions, the towns sided with the Pretender. The mind of the countryside was divided; the peasants found themselves caught up in a tangle of issues beyond their understanding. The country suggested a patchwork quilt, pattern and color at war with one another.

Chapter XII

Who was the young man sprung out of obscurity into the luxurious climate of a wealthy Lithuanian household? Legendary details are many, but few if any of them can be believed. Supposed to have been an illegitimate son of a petty landowner at Galitz, the Pretender is said to have been brought up in a Romanov household in Moscow. His piety having developed, he was said to have become a novice at a monastery and to have fled from it when someone disclosed his "true" identity. But what was his true identity? His future courses considered, it is much more likely that the youth recoiled from the daily hardships of monastic routine. In Muscovite abbeys a novice's life was not an easy one. Burdened with laborious manual tasks and lengthy sessions of prayer when he could not so much as lean against a pillar, he was fed on a pittance "to mortify the flesh," and slept on straw in dorters which were not heated even in the cruel northern winters, and in any case his hours of sleep were few. After early Mass the novices were sent out to work, breakfast being considered a sinful indulgence. The dinner bell rang at eleven in the morning, but the half hour in the refectory hardly appeased their hunger: thin gruel, boiled turnips, and an apple were not much of a meal. For supper they would get vegetable stew and rye bread, with water to drink. On feast days they were treated to a herring, roasted eggs, or a pie. On vigils they got no supper at all. If such, then, had been the Pretender's early background, it would be easy to understand the reasons for his flight, an action heavily penalized by the laws of both Church and state.

But was the pseudo-Dimitry (*Lzhé-Dimitry*, as he came to be known) ever in a monastery? Nobody can tell.

There is a scene in Pushkin's drama *Boris Godunov* in which constables sent out by Boris to search for the Pretender discover him in a countryside tavern and he escapes by leaping through a window. But the episode, however forcefully told, is no more than an echo of an ancient legend.

Fables and legends apart, some facts stand out clearly. The Pretender, whatever his origins, must have had some noble blood in him. No humbly born vagabond would have been welcomed at the castle of a Lithuanian magnate. Again, whatever his obscure beginnings, the young man must have had opportunities to acquire some education. He knew his letters. He understood Latin.

The Pretender also knew Muscovy. He spoke the language like a native, and he knew the customs. He knew what had happened at Uglich in 1591.

But the Pretender's other accomplishments rather war against a Muscovite upbringing. He had a fine voice and he could sing, but he did not sing songs he would have learned in Muscovy. He danced well and paid delicate court to his host's daughter, Marina Mnishek. No nobly born Muscovite ever danced. To pay court to a young lady was in Muscovite eyes something like putting a saddle on a cow. They never courted. Their brides were chosen by their parents, and no son of Ivan the Terrible would have dreamed of entering the Roman Catholic Church. The Pretender did so in order to marry Marina Mnishek and, even more importantly, to be assured of financial aid from the King of Poland.

He was adroitly elusive about his earlier years. The Pretender's allusions to his late "father" moved the Lithuanians. His repeated longing to reach Moscow and there see his "mother" again left them in tears. Prince Mnishek was enraptured to think of his daughter becoming the Czarina of the mighty Muscovy.

But an invasion demanded money and men. The Pretender was penniless and, with the exception of a magnate here and there, Lithuania was not a rich country. Her men were eager enough to follow the Pretender, but they had to be mounted, armed, and

81

fed. On its own, Mnishek's great treasury could not support the expenditure. There remained neighboring Poland, wealthy, cultured, and studiedly aloof.

At a banquet in Lithuania the Pretender made his claim public. He admitted that he was poor, but, he argued, that would be remedied once he ascended the Muscovite throne. Toward the end of his speech he declared his resolve to see Lithuania and Poland united to Muscovy, thus bringing his "father's" country into line with Western culture. The Lithuanians were enchanted.

The Pretender's carefully worded speech duly reached Kracow. King Sigismund of Poland, who at the beginning had doubted the stranger's claims, now changed his mind. He felt tempted. A union of Muscovy and Poland had once been no more than a fantastic dream. Now it seemed a not too distant reality. Sigismund sent messengers to Lithuania, their saddlebags bulging with gold, and he promised to raise an army.

But there were delays. The Polish nobles were in no hurry to respond to their king's resolve. They could not be certain of the outcome. They did not know enough about Prince Mnishek's guest, and the Polish scouts reported that Muscovy itself was a seething caldron.

King Sigismund sent more money, but the Pretender needed men as well. What Lithuanians showed themselves ready to follow him were not enough. The Pretender could count on two or three thousand men under arms, and whatever his lack of military experience, he saw clearly that such a small host would hardly pave his way to Moscow. So he lingered at his host's castle, married Marina Mnishek in the private chapel, and waited for developments.

These came suddenly. The story of Ivan's "son" having been rescued from murderers at Uglich soon reached the southern and eastern reaches of Muscovy. The Cossacks and others acclaimed the Pretender and moved northward. Blessed by the Jesuits and Dominicans of Lithuania, secure of his bride's adoration and her father's support, the Pretender rode out on his crusade. Victory after victory paved his way. Peasants who had never heard of Uglich came out by the hundreds to shout a deafening welcome: "Long live Czar Dimitry." The Pretender would stop, address them kindly and encouragingly, and promise them freedom from taxes and an end to landowners' oppression. The children, led by the elder of a village, presented him with bunches of spring flowers, honey, and branches of willow. The Pretender's smile was a reward they had not expected.

The Muscovite armies drew back or declared themselves for "Czar Dimitry." One day in the late spring of 1605 he rode into Moscow. The Dowager Czarina, Maria Nagaya, left her cloister and publicly acknowledged him as her "true son." Their reunion moved thousands to tears. Maria rode into the Kremlin, a palace she never thought of entering again. The assembled household prostrated themselves before her and her "son." The Pretender was led to the Czar's apartments, there to be served a sumptuous banquet. Not a dish was brought in but the men knelt to present it. He tasted the food rather reluctantly and in the end told one of the stewards that he was not accustomed to the Muscovite way of overspicing every dish. The gentlemen in attendance watched him. He made the sign of the cross in a foreign manner and the sharp Muscovite ear caught a strange accent or two in his speech. "But that," they whispered to one another, "may be due to his having been brought up across the border."

Yet the Dowager Czarina had "recognized" the stranger. Members of the hierarchy and the boyar Duma saw that there was no choice but to acknowledge his claim. "Dimitry" swore on the Gospel book that he would keep the Orthodox faith, uphold the law, and govern the country in the spirit of his "father." So they had him crowned czar at the Assumption Cathedral in the Kremlin.

Chapter XIII

The country brooded. Everyone longed for peace and order after the ravages of the great famine. But peace stayed away and there seemed to be nobody to restore order. Monks, military stragglers, and vagabonds wandered from town to town, from village to village, repeating what gossip they had heard in Moscow. It was by no means idle gossip. Little by little, the earlier enthusiastic welcome for Czar Ivan's "son" died down. Harrows, plows, sickles, spades were laid aside. Peasants took to plundering the neighboring manors and hid their booty under the earthen floors of their huts. In the towns, the bureaucrats, with no directions and no wages, turned into gangs to search for food and clothing. A clerk's wife, accustomed to a hodden-gray kirtle, an apron of rough sacking, and a clumsily cut blouse, could be seen sporting a bright red velvet *saráfan*, a blue silk skirt, and

green shoes embroidered with silver beads. But finery did not slake hunger. Food began growing scarce. Butchers', fishmongers', and grain merchants' stores were drained through raids, and no further supplies came in.

A rumor might start that in a field some five versts away five cows had been seen grazing. A crowd armed with axes, hatchets, and cleavers would rush to the field, kill the animals, and hack at the carcasses in such frenzy that a clumsily held ax would cleave a neighbor's bent head in two. Such spoils usually ended in bloodshed.

The clergy were helpless. Most of the belfries stood

silent, and parishioners stayed away from church. All the ancient traditions became so many wisps of straw.

The people did not say their prayers. They neglected the field labor and other tasks. But they listened to rumors because they were curious, bewildered, and frightened. When someone spread the news that far away in Moscow they were planning a union with Poland, the peasants' wrath flamed high. Poland—their immemorial enemy! They had no idea how far or how near Poland was. That did not matter. A crowd surrounded the man who had dared to bring such an appalling story. They cursed him and dragged him to the nearest river. "Here is your Poland for you!" they shouted as they tossed him into the current and watched him drown, imagining that they had thus removed the peril.

In a village near Vologda a mysterious pest attacked what few fowls remained. The priest's wife heard of the disease and forbade the eating of the birds. "It is a poison," she said. "The birds must be killed and burned."

The village listened. They knew nothing about any fowl pest and they decided that the *popádia* (priest's wife) had invented the story to rob them of their poultry. The priest happened to be away. The folk got together, made for the priest's house, and set it on fire. The woman and her three small children perished in the flames.

It seemed as if the countryside had taken a plunge back into remote centuries.

Chapter XIV

Matters were hardly better in the capital. The government could not govern. Trade narrowed down to a trickle. In Lithuania, Prince Mnishek kept his daughter at home and sent messenger after messenger to his son-in-law to assure him that Marina would come as soon as conditions were quieter in Muscovy. King Sigismund of Poland, annoyed that the project of union seemed to have reached a stalemate, sent no more money. But Czar Dimitry was having the time of his life. The Kremlin treasury crypts made him leap for joy: cups, platters, dishes, jugs, and goblets of gold, encrusted with diamonds, pearls, and amethysts; great oaken coffers filled with gold coins from many countries; priceless curios, including ten sets of chessmen, a present to Czar Ivan from the Shah of Persia, the chessmen carved of jade and ivory and studded with precious stones of fabulous value. The palace steward led Czar Dimitry down the narrow stairs and had all the torches lit in the old crypts. The Czar ran from one coffer to another, clapped his hands, pirouetted, and shouted that he was the sovereign of the richest country in the world. He tossed gems into the stewards' hands, ordered a stupendous banquet, and told the men that, having married the loveliest woman in Europe, he would now load her with rubies, pearls, and diamonds. On leaving the crypts, Dimitry demanded that all the keys should be handed over to him.

A few days later came the vigil of an important Orthodox feast. Dimitry duly attended the long Vespers. The vigil proper, as far as abstinence was concerned, began after the service, and supper was to be served at nine in the evening. To the undisguised horror of the household, Dimitry, already known to be fussy in matters of food, chose the meal himself. It was to begin with a veal broth and include a broiled goose, among other things. The chief butler dared not protest. Prince Danila Miloslavsky, one of the oldest and most courageous of the boyars, broke the etiquette for once and said to Dimitry that neither meat nor eggs could be eaten on a vigil, according to Church law. "I was brought up in the West," was the reply. "There are different usages there and I am accustomed to them."

He had his goose that evening and did not know that the first lines of a death warrant were being shaped in the minds of his attendants. They whispered

among themselves. The muttering swept through the gates of the Kremlin and seeped into the humblest corner of the capital. "Whom have we got for a czar?" people began asking one another and were unable to answer. The military took to murmuring. "Crowned by the Patriarch and all, and eats meat on a vigil! What manner of a czar is he?" Their indignation grew to a danger point when a group of Polish noblemen, accompanied by their ladies and retinues, swooped upon Moscow. Dimitry was delighted. There followed banquets and masked balls at the Kremlin. Many a treasured necklace from the crypts went to

90

adorn the Polish ladies. Their husbands' attitude toward the Muscovite noblemen was an insulting mixture of condescension and contempt. They were provocative with their frequent allusions to the approaching union of Poland with Muscovy—with Poland in the forefront. "We shall fight you yet," said a gray-haired boyar. "You are not Slavs. You are Latins, steeped in the devil's lore." "What an unmannerly joke," said Dimitry when he heard of it. "But what else did you expect? They are barbarians. I mean to force culture on them."

The astounding fact is that, during the sessions of the Duma, Dimitry shed his buffoon's trappings. He observed the least detail of the intricate ceremonial. He gave audiences to ambassadors and answered their speeches in faultless Latin. He dealt deftly with foreign affairs and seldom alluded to Lithuania or to the union with Poland. He discussed a lasting peace with Sweden as an expert, and he assured the imperial ambassadors of his good will.

But having left the throne room, Dimitry hurried back to the privacy of his own apartments, where he was at liberty to wax eloquent about his "father." As often as not, Dimitry plunged into reminiscences that were absurdly unreal, for Ivan IV's youngest child was an infant at the time of Ivan's death in 1584.

In Lithuania, Prince Mnishek, reassured by the presence of so many Poles in the capital of Muscovy, sent Marina to Moscow. She traveled as behoved a czarina, with a great retinue of ladies and male attendants, followed by a host of priests, monks, and friars. Her progress to Moscow was received in silence, but there were no ugly incidents.

Dimitry and a crowd of Polish nobles met Marina outside the gates of Moscow. The inhabitants of the capital stayed indoors. She leaped into her husband's arms, unaware that her arrival would hasten a national crisis. The streets of the capital were empty. The couple rode into the Kremlin. Polish ladies and gentlewomen waited on Marina in her apartments. Her husband's gifts, filched from the Kremlin crypts, lay everywhere: necklaces, tiaras, bracelets, rings, bejeweled mirrors—the low-ceilinged rooms sparkled with diamonds, rubies, sapphires, opals, emeralds. Marina danced for joy when her women dressed her for dinner. She gave orders that one of the rooms was to be fitted up as a Catholic chapel. She glided into the supper room and grace was intoned in Latin by her Dominican confessor. The last dainty eaten, husband and wife vanished into their private apartments, no Muscovites being allowed to attend them.

Moscow watched closely and Moscow was not alone. Up and down Muscovy there were protesting voices. The whispers grew that the man crowned as czar was an impostor. His wife, decked out in the ancient Muscovite jewelry, was a Latin whore. "If Moscow would rise," muttered the peasantry, "we are there to a man. We will not be sold to the Latins."

The Kremlin idyl lasted a few weeks. From her cloister the Dowager Czarina Maria, wholly neglected by her "son," was the first to raise her voice. Sobbing and wringing her hands, Ivan IV's last wife appeared at the abbey gates and publicly acknowledged her mistake. Her real son, she said, had been killed at Uglich in 1591. "The Devil," wailed the Dowager Czarina, "prompted me to lie."

The confession, however hysterical and inarticulate, leaped over the capital. Here then was the final proof of all the suspicions. A czar? An impostor, an alien, a marauder, a glutton, a drunkard, and worse. There was no longer any question of rival factions at court. Conspiracy? Yes, a conspiracy soon grew to stir into fury every peasant in Muscovy who had heard about a goose eaten on a vigil eve.

A day came when the Kremlin Palace was crowded with Poles, their servants and guards all heavily armed. In her own rooms, Marina, helped by her ladies, was busily packing gold, silver, and jewelry, hiding fabulous pearls and diamonds under collars, inside belts, between the double linings of cloaks and kirtles, in preparation for flight. In the end, the so-called Czarina of Muscovy and her attendants, dressed in rough peasant clothes, found two Poles to bring them through an underground passage under the gates of the Kremlin. Marina is supposed to have fled southwest, but nobody troubled about her.

The Poles found themselves in an enemy country. Bribing to right and left, they galloped off into safety, not a thought about the "Czar" in their minds. An oddly assorted host of conspirators found the palace undefended. Even the scullions in the kitchens did not interfere. The Pretender was killed instantly, his body dragged out and flung into a bonfire. Later, his ashes were thrown into the Moskva, and the people of Moscow danced for joy to be rid of the alien.

So did the folk in the country. The Pretender, having reigned for about a year, had never shown any concern for them. They decided he had been a traitor, always trying to win the favor of Muscovy's enemies, Poland and Lithuania. Stories ran rife that his Polish hangers-on had pillaged the Moscow churches, that cartloads of gold and other treasures had been sent to the western border, that the Pretender's "fancy lady" had decked herself out in diamonds from head to foot and had dared bring her accursed Latin monks and friars into the Moscow sanctuaries.

But the killing of the Pretender brought no peace to the country. Muscovy was like a sick man tossing about on his bed.

City rose against city, village against village. Thick forests became lairs for brigands. There were no authorities to check the collapse of law and order.

Chapter XV

In the summer of 1606 the Duma held a tumultuous session which went on for hours. Their business was to elect one of themselves czar. In the end a candidate was found in Prince Vassily Shuyskie. When crowned, he faced a bankrupt nation, an empty treasury, an angrily divided Duma, and a vast country on the brink of total insurrection. A genius would have seen it as a Titan's task, but Czar Vassily was no genius.

Among other cities, Tver flatly refused to recognize his election. The working classes at Pskov attacked gentlefolk and merchants, massacring them to a man. Mutinies broke out along the banks of the Volga and other rivers. Neither the peasants nor the urban folk knew what they were fighting about. If they heard anyone shouting "We need the National Assembly," they would scream themselves hoarse: *"Sobór! So-*

bór!"—the Assembly, the Assembly—though none understood why the Assembly was needed, or what it would do.

With the approval of the Duma, Czar Vassily sent what military were in Moscow to deal with the peasant rebellions. But the Muscovite soldiery, too, were divided in mind. Some went willingly, but the majority, detesting the idea of fighting their own people, moved slowly, complaining that there were real enemies for them to march against. Great numbers of men under arms threw in their lot with the rebel peasants, and gloried in it. The lower ranks came from peasant stock, and it was a happy change to turn back to peasant labor. When ordered to move farther south to Kazan and Astrakhan, they bluntly refused, saying: "Let the Tartar meddle in that business."

Polish spies lost little time in reporting on the soldiers marching from Moscow. King Sigismund's reaction was prompt: a strong and well-disciplined Polish army moved eastward toward the borders of Muscovy. Vassily appealed to Sweden for help, and a huge army of Swedish and Baltic mercenaries moved to the defense of Moscow. Sigismund's counter-measure was swift: he ordered his regiments to lay siege to Smolensk.

The people of Moscow, terrified of falling into the hands of the Poles, welcomed the Swedes vociferously. But the Swedish army mercenaries insisted on getting a regular wage. The unhappy Vassily had not a single silver ruble in his treasury. Members of the Duma used all their eloquence to explain the national plight to the

Swedish commanders, who replied that no explanations would satisfy their men : they wanted money and not excuses. The Swedes left Moscow, found the Polish army, and joined forces with Moscow's enemies at Smolensk. Polish purses were full. The mercenaries were paid well and promptly, and it mattered little to them for whom they were fighting.

Smolensk, with its markets and huge storehouses, promised rich booty, but the people, well prepared for a siege, had no intention of a quick surrender. The siege dragged on and on, to King Sigismund's displeasure.

In the West, the Kings of England, France, and Spain, to say nothing of the Emperor and the rulers of various Italian states, had as good as written Muscovy off their maps. One question remained : Which country was the most likely to swallow up Muscovy? Would it be Poland or Sweden? The West, remaining rigorously neutral, preferred Sweden. Yet the Duma in Moscow thought otherwise.

No more than three years later, the same men who had elected Vassily czar removed him from the throne and forced him to become a monk in a remote monastery in northern Muscovy. Vassily was permitted to utter his "abdication." In all truth, he must have been relieved to lay down a burden he could not carry. At least a cloister promised peace, which was unlikely to be found under the palace roof. Vassily was such a pallid character that the effect of his very brief reign was as insignificant to the Muscovites as a falling leaf.

Once again the throne was vacant, and the countryside was flung from one chaos into another. Peasants understood little if anything of governmental activities. Immediacies gripped their minds: no fairs, no peddlers, no markets, the increase of brigandage and similar evils. If a harvest was bountiful, where would the peasant get his grain ground when so many neighboring mills were beyond repair? If some pest or other attacked his cattle and they died, he and his kin would roast the tainted meat, convinced that fire "cleansed all manner of evil," and feasted at their pleasure. But fire did not cleanse, and many died.

The peasant body was well used to physical hardship and dangers. But the peasant mind was hopeless when it came to the unraveling of political intrigue. He dimly felt that the chaos he lived in was born of disunity, and a peasant knew but one symbol of unity: an anointed, truly Orthodox czar. A peasant, knowing nothing of autocracy, firmly held that under God a czar could do all things. The peasant mind could not grasp theological tenets. A countryman lived by a blind faith hedged about with familiar outward observations: to attend church services with frequent prostration, to kiss the cross and the ikons, to use three fingers when making the sign of the cross—such were the evidences of true Orthodoxy and within them lay that mysterious unity, imaged in the czar's person, which held the country together.

Now they knew that they had no czar and, for them, all the shortages, the evils, and the horrors of chaos derived from the empty throne.

Chapter XVI

The Duma spent weeks in futile deliberations. In the end, a faction leaped into prominence which declared once again that the only salvation lay in the union of Muscovy and Poland. The latter, however, had to be won over. The most tempting bait would be the offer of the Muscovite crown to Prince Wladislas, King Sigismund's son and heir. The opposing factions murmured their disapproval, but they had no alternative to suggest. The pro-Polish members went on pressing their point. Such a measure, they argued, would hold Sweden in check, cripple the savage designs of the Crimean Tartars, revive Western respect for the Slav nation, and bring prosperity to their own unhappy country.

The opposing factions gave in on condition that Prince Wladislas should enter the Orthodox Church. The condition was fantastic: the Prince, brought up

99

by Jesuits and stanchly grounded in his own faith, would never forsake it for any throne in the world. But the Duma brushed aside this obvious difficulty and appointed an embassy to ride to Kracow.

When the country heard the news, it rose in fury. In Moscow itself the hierarchy kept prudently aloof, but the common people did not. One frenzied mob after another stormed the gates of the Kremlin, shouting that they would raze the whole place to the ground if the young Prince so much as set foot on the lowest step of the Red Porch. What military there were in the capital joined the mobs. Farther south, the various Cossack groups rejected the idea of an alien sovereign. Their spokesman rode to Moscow, declaring that Marina, still in hiding, had a son by "Czar Dimitry." The Cossacks believed him to be Ivan the Terrible's grandson and they swore they would owe allegiance to none other. The situation became a tragicomedy, for nobody knew Marina's whereabouts. Even if found, it was doubtful that, having gone through so many horrors in Moscow, she would have been willing to surrender her son into the keeping of the Duma.

The peasants heard of this development. They did not go to the capital. They were busy sharpening their sickles and hatchets. That would be their answer to the "Latin usurper." When in a village near Kostroma the priest tearfully implored the parishioners to remember that the young Prince would enter the Orthodox Church, the people replied with a rude native equivalent of "Tell it to the marines."

100

The crisis was resolved in a manner nobody had expected.

King Sigismund was certainly in favor of the union, but he meant to rule the two countries. When the Muscovite embassy reached Kracow and put its proposals to him, he imprisoned them all, including their leader, the monk Philaret, who had once been Fedor Romanov.

Sigismund's next move was to order his army to march east and besiege Moscow; the siege was to be raised only when the Muscovites accepted him as czar. But the Muscovites, having spurned Prince Wladislas, had small use for his father. They remembered the noblemen in Marina's retinue and their undisguised contempt for all they saw at the Kremlin. A Muscovite prince, his pedigree going back to the ninth century, would say to another of the same rank: "Have you forgotten that they expected *us* to fill their goblets at dinner? And *our* sons were ordered to pull off their boots and fetch their shoes! The Polish women were there, wearing clothes of that shameless Western cut, their faces were unveiled, and they crossed themselves in the Latin fashion."

For once the peasantry were at one with the boyars. How could the Poles be Slavs when they were of an alien faith? Gallows were too good for them, said the peasants.

The Duma faction, having suggested Prince Wladislas as a sovereign, backed out and kept quiet. They attended the appointed meetings but they had nothing

to say. King Sigismund's army approached from the west. Swedish mercenaries, having fallen out with the Poles and Lithuanians, marched toward Novgorod and marauded there. On reflection, the Cossack groups retreated south. In a forest glade they held a primitive council of war. Should it be their business to search for a young woman, an alien by blood and religion, the Marina who had brought nothing but trouble? No, decided the Cossacks, their chief concern was to rescue the capital. They turned northward, but they did not reach Moscow in time to prevent the Poles from sacking the city.

A few *strielzy* regiments were still in the capital, but even their commanders had no clear plan of action. The roads to Moscow were blocked. Her markets were empty, and nobody knew where more supplies would come from. A fervent monk from Chudov Abbey assured what listeners he could muster that God's bounty would not fail. "God's own word says so. His people were starving and sweet manna fell down from heaven."

But no manna came to cover the squares and streets of the capital. Nobly bred women and merchants' wives, spades in their hands, started digging for what edibles still grew in the back gardens. The humbler folk would fight for a hare's carcass, a bag of mildewed corn, or a bunch of rotten carrots. The threat of famine drew nearer. In a nobleman's mansion there had been forty-six servants. Thirty had taken French leave. Sixteen were left. "There are our daughters' dowries," said the wife to her husband. "But who will buy jewels, fine linen, and velvet today?"

The lady did not know it, but there were some who would. The seventeenth-century black market became part of the national life. Strangers, even foreigners, wormed their way into the capital. Barter, concluded in dark slummy corners, came into its own—on a pitiful scale, because few of the poorer inhabitants had much to offer, and food came in small bundles, the contents unlikely to satisfy the needs of even a hovel.

In the end, King Sigismund's army, victualing trains in the rear, passed through the city gates. They did not come as allies but as conquerors. The starving population did not concern them. The Muscovite military fled, but from many a neighboring village peasants rushed to the rescue of Moscow's sanctuaries. The gesture, if gallant, proved futile: not a man was left to turn back to his homestead, and the ancient capital lay at the mercy of the Poles.

These were grim days. The Poles lost no time in bringing in the curfew and martial law. The Duma was dissolved. The invaders crowded into the Kremlin and recruited princes of Rurik descent, wool merchants, clergy, and cobblers into their service—chiefly for domestic tasks. Lower ranks of the enemy host were free to wander about the city, killing, burning, and pillaging at their pleasure, until the news of the Cossacks' approach made them run to the Kremlin and mount guard at the gates. The commanders assured the men that King Sigismund had promised reinforcements and that there were enough supplies in the Kremlin.

In reality, the Poles were trapped behind those high stone walls. No reinforcements could have run the gauntlet of the Cossacks' vigilance. Indeed, there had been no promises from Kracow. Not a single Polish unit was marching to the support of its compatriots.

Chapter XVII

The invaders, caught in a trap, had a trump card to play. In an underground cell of Chudov Abbey in the Kremlin they had hidden their most important prisoner: Patriarch Hermogen, an old and frail man, who shared his imprisonment with a chaplain and a couple of clerks. The Poles knew that Hermogen wielded great influence over the people and they took care that the conditions of his imprisonment were as bearable as possible. What few guards there were treated him with respect. Adequate meals were brought in. The four prisoners were supplied with candles, kindling, books, and writing materials. One or another of the Polish noblemen paid a daily call, inquired after the Patriarch's health, and spoke airily about the "improving conditions" in the capital. The old man listened, too courteous to contradict.

The Poles had drawn up a plan. After several tentative approaches, they laid it before him. The entire country, they said, had unbounded trust in the Patriarch. There was no more Duma, but he remained. He had writing materials at his disposal. A few words from him, they said, would convince the country that a union with Poland would be to its advantage. There would not be the least interference with the country's faith. Its cathedrals, abbeys, and village churches would remain Orthodox. Once the union became fact, peace and prosperity would flow over the country like a river in full spate. Generations would bless the Patriarch's name.

It would have to be a convincing paper, said the Poles, and they realized that the Patriarch could not compose it in a hurry. A few weeks, even a couple of months, would serve the purpose.

Hermogen listened attentively. When the Poles left him, they did not know that they had given him an idea for a plan of his own.

He did not believe his jailers' stories about "improving conditions" in the capital. Still less could he, great churchman and statesman that he was, admit the possibility of an advantageous union with Poland. But there was no need for his visitors to wax eloquent about his influence. Hermogen knew that he had the people's trust. He prayed that the message he was about to frame would stir his unhappy country and guide her people toward the right path.

Nobody knows how the following events came about. The Patriarch's guards were certainly few and negligent. Most likely, either Hermogen's chaplain or one of the clerks succeeded in enlisting the aid of what few loyal Muscovites still remained at the Kremlin.

Quietly, unhurriedly, the old man started on his task. The paper he intended to write had to be brief, simple, convincing, fiery. The clerks, taking advantage of the privacy afforded them, made one copy after another. By a method unknown to us, those leaflets left Chudov Abbey, were slipped out of the Kremlin, smuggled across the city gates to travel north and south, east and west, all over Muscovy for the few literates to read them to the illiterate masses.

Hermogen urged everybody to turn back on all dissensions, to muster together, to drive the foreign invader out of the country, then to call a *Sobor*—a national assembly—and to elect a czar of their own faith and blood. He ended by calling God's blessing on his flock and signed himself their "unworthy and humble servant, Hermogen." After the leaflets had left Chudov Abbey, he and his three companions could do nothing but pray that some of them would reach men willing and able to answer the appeal.

Such was Hermogen's work. It also proved to be his death warrant. Again we cannot tell who betrayed him, but at least one of the leaflets did not leave the Kremlin: it went to the palace and reached the Poles. They read it in fury. Guards were sent to Chudov Abbey and led away the chaplain and the clerks—presumably to their death. The old man was kneeling at

prayer when the guards returned. They stripped the
cell of the last vestige of comfort; they cleared the
table, which was set for supper, extinguished the candles, and left, bolting and barring the door of the cell.
The frail old man was left to starve to death.

Chapter XVIII

The martyred Patriarch's work did not die with him. In the autumn of 1611, the Polish marauders still held the Kremlin. Some of the Cossacks having withdrawn, the Poles spread themselves all over the capital. There were casual hand-to-hand fights whenever a Pole came on a Cossack, and the Moskva, the Yauza, and other lesser streams often ran crimson. Yet, with anarchy at its worst throughout the country, individual cases of violence meant little. Town dwellers and country folk reached that dull gray point where nothing mattered. If you were not killed, either starvation or disease took you. Nobody could fight such enemies.

By mere chance a leaflet of Hermogen's reached Nijny-Novgorod on the Volga. Once one of the richest cities in the land, famous for its markets and its great annual fair, Nijny-Novgorod might well have become a churchyard if it had not been for the stubbornness of its inhabitants. Drawn into the national vortex, often hungry and cold, forced to watch the terrible evidences of the *Smuta* on their right hand and on their left, the people nevertheless refused to lose hope.

Someone had the good sense to carry the Patriarch's leaflet to one of the most upright citizens of the city, a man known and loved for his justice and generosity, one Kuzma Minin, a butcher by trade. He read the leaflet carefully and saw his duty quite clearly. By virtue of his municipal position, it was not difficult for Minin to summon a public meeting in the largest square of Nijny-Novgorod. Standing on the cathedral steps, Minin read Hermogen's appeal to the immense crowd, and added a few words of his own : "Orthodox people, Moscow must be saved."

The people's reaction was immediate and spontaneous. The capital and indeed the whole country must be wrested out of the enemy's clutches. A local magnate, Prince Pozharsky, was singled out as leader, and recruitment started without delay. Noblemen, clergy, smallholders, clerks, merchants, peddlers, artisans, and peasants hurried to join the host. Neither Pozharsky nor Minin thought anything about differences of rank : a princeling rubbed shoulders with a tattered fisherman, a priest shared his wooden cross with a locksmith. One and all accepted the challenge : it was *obtchée délo*—everyone's business.

The surrounding countryside down to the humblest village responded vigorously. Pozharsky and Minin could not tell if bigger centers farther away would be ready to join them, but nothing deterred them. Nijny-Novgorod was infused with a burning enthusiasm, a hunger for unity. Having decided that money would be needed for the expedition, Minin turned his big house into a collection center. A shoemaker was not ashamed to put down three or four coppers next to the emerald necklace of some magnate's wife. Parents readily gave up their daughters' dowries. Every action bore a touch of the miraculous. Three gangs of brigands sought out Prince Pozharsky, knelt before him, and begged to be admitted into the army, swearing "by the cross" that they would abide by the law.

Recruitment went on. Early in 1612 the leaders knew they could start on their march northward. One February morning, Pozharsky, preceded by the ikon of Our Lady of Pokrová, led his men out of Nijny-Novgorod.

The season was hardly propitious for the venture. Winter came to an early end that year. Roads, neglected for years, were nothing but slush, mud, and floods running furiously from swollen rivers and streams. When a road went through a forest, the way would be blocked by gigantic trees uprooted during the winter storms. Often enough, the men plodded through mud and slush to come to a village that was a broken huddle of hovels, its wooden church a charred ruin—evidence of the anarchy which gripped the country. Pozharsky would not halt. What help could be offered to skeletons—men, women, and children

111

who had died of starvation and whose bones had been picked clean by wild beasts? The men marched on, conscious of still another notch in the tally against the enemy.

Spring was well behind them when the immense army, its morale unshaken by the hardships of the long march, reached the foothills of Sparrow Hills south of Moscow. The woods were full of life. Larches were changing their wintry black for pale gold; elms had already put out their shy young greenery. Encouraging scents came from the soil and the trees, and every dawn began with bird song.

Wisely, Prince Pozharsky and the other commanders decided to give the men a rest before the last and the most arduous task awaiting them. It was still too early in the year for wildings, berries, and mushrooms to be found in the woods, but the men managed to snare or shoot hares and rabbits to replenish their stores, and in the streams the water ran sweet and clear. So soft was the weather that they rested in the open air. There came no gusts of wind, and cooks were able to bake rye *lepéshky*, a rough kind of pancake, on improvised braziers. Evening crept into the silken dark of a spring night as Vespers were chanted by the priests. The men stretched out gratefully on dry ground, the mind of each absorbed by the idea that, all the hardship and uncertainties notwithstanding, they had reached the outskirts of the capital.

Chapter XIX

The months to follow tested the Poles' strength and resolve to the utmost. They knew they had lost the game. No reinforcements from either Poland or Lithuania reached them, and Sweden did not intervene. Trapped in the capital, with hunger fast approaching, the Poles grew aware that the army battering at Moscow's walls was but a forerunner of what was to come: behind those ranks stood a whole country determined to chase the aliens off its soil.

"But we meant nothing except good," moaned the Polish nobles to one another. "The union of our kingdom with theirs would have led these blockheads to a paradise. But they were born barbarians and they will die as such."

Week by week, month by month, the bloody siege continued. Every piece of Polish artillery was mounted on the walls. When cannon balls gave out, the Poles began prizing huge cobbles out of the streets to fire instead, emptying caldrons of boiling pitch and tossing bunches of flaming straw over the walls. Pozharsky's casualties were many, but his men never wavered. Their own artillery was negligible, but they were master bowmen and pikemen.

In the early autumn of 1612 Pozharsky's men entered the city. The Poles, having expected no mercy, found none. The last alien either killed or expelled, Pozharsky's army knew that Moscow again belonged to Muscovy.

Alas! Little of the beauty was left to welcome them. The Kremlin sanctuaries were hideously pillaged and grossly dishallowed, the Poles having stabled their horses in some of the cathedrals. A loyal survivor of the siege brought Pozharsky's men to Chudov Abbey. In an underground cell they found the skeleton of Patriarch Hermogen and gave him the burial due his rank. What few survivors were left could speak of nothing but the inhuman cruelty of the Poles. Kuzma Minin distributed among them what edibles there were. The downtrodden, terrified, half-starved population, dumbly grateful for the bounty, asked no questions. The hateful enemy had been driven out. What more was there to expect?

But there was much more.

The enemy had gone, but the evidences of the occupation remained. The Kremlin palaces had been stripped bare. So had the mansions and churches. The Cossacks had robbed the former but spared the latter.

Not so the Poles, to whom a "schismatic church" was a place to pillage and dishallow. Outside the Kremlin walls, whole streets of wooden houses were so many charred stumps. Grass and weeds carpeted the once busy marketplaces. There were no fish in the Moscow rivers, the waters polluted by corpses and garbage.

Pozharsky's great army stayed on in the ravaged capital. The artisans among the volunteers were directed toward the jobs which had been theirs in the years of peace. The inhabitants, some of whom had never wielded a saw or a hammer, flocked to join the experts. Outside, the roads, whatever their sorry condition, were safe enough. From the north and the east, peasants and peddlers drove in laden carts to ease the shortages in the capital. A wool merchant's wife felt triumphant when she purchased some eggs and a round of rough country cheese. "I have paid for them. I did not steal them, and there is nobody to rob me of them," she said aloud for a whole square to hear.

Even though the enemy had fled westward, Pozharsky took no chances. The western and northwestern reaches of Moscow were guarded day and night. At the time, neither Minin nor Pozharsky realized that the story of their march to Moscow had winged over the West, that leaders in Scandinavia, Germany, the Low Countries, and even farther south were astounded by the faultless strategy of the expedition. Muscovy, all its scars notwithstanding, was a country again, not a desert given over to marauders' violent whims.

There was more for the two leaders to do. Houses

might be rebuilt, women might no longer fret about the empty larder shelves, and roads might be comparatively safe. But that was not enough. The men of Nijny-Novgorod had not endured all their hardships just to place a rye loaf on someone's table. A lasting and rewarding unity needed a unifying symbol. A czar of native blood and faith must be anointed and crowned at the Assumption Cathedral in the Kremlin.

Hosts of accredited messengers left Moscow and rode to every town, however big or small, in the country. By Christmas 1612 the capital was crowded with representatives sent to attend the *Sobor*, or National Assembly. For one purpose only would they meet : the choice of the future czar. They met in the biggest hall of the Kremlin. A forester shared a bench with a magnate, a small landowner, a peddler, a butcher, a mercer, and a clerk. At the head of the crowded benches, on a hurriedly built, uncarpeted, unadorned dais, sat Pozharsky, Kuzma Minin, and a few of their closest intimates who had been with them through the arduous campaign. A clerk, a long sheet of paper in his hands, crouched at the end of a trestle. The hierarchy in their long white and black robes sat facing him. The first sitting began with a prayer to the Holy Ghost, the Comforter, to enlighten their minds and to lead them toward a right decision for the future prosperity of the country.

Then Prince Pozharsky made a brief speech, telling the Assembly they had but one point to settle. Muscovy without a czar was like a rudderless ship. Theirs was

the choice. A list of likely candidates would be read out to them. The votes would be counted. The czar-elect must be chosen by the will of the people. Then Pozharsky sat down and the clerk stood up.

The list was headed by men of the renowned Rurik descent, sons and grandsons of those who had perished during the persecutions of Ivan the Terrible. One great name after another rang in the hall. The repre-sentatives remained immobile. The session went on and on. The day was closing fast. A hurriedly con-trived meal was served to the Assembly. Everyone ate and drank in silence. Winter shadows crept in, and tallow candles were lit. The list of likely noblemen was coming to an end. The clerk's tired voice mentioned a few more names. The Assembly remained impassive. Then came the name Michael Romanov.

Instantly everybody stirred. Those who were familiar with the surname shook their heads and shouted an emphatic no. Those who had never heard of the candidate followed the others' example. A portly merchant from Tver launched into a narrative of reasons against the election. Michael Romanov was far too young. They wanted a czar, not a dubious regency. Was the lad not the son of Fedor Romanov, Philaret in religion, who had led a Muscovy embassy to Kracow to offer the crown to King Sigismund's heir, Prince Wladislas? Why, they might as well have a Dane or a Swede for czar. Philaret was still in Kracow. There were rumors that he had been imprisoned by King Sigismund. Was there any truth in that? If they were to elect a Romanov, they might well expect another Polish invasion. King Sigismund was cunning. He bided his time. It would be far better, concluded the Tver merchant, to offer the crown to someone of unstained Rurik descent.

Assenting voices broke out here and there. The turmoil in the hall grew. Someone conveniently remembered that three or four Polish spies had been caught and vigorously dealt with in Moscow. Most likely there were others hiding within the Kremlin. Thus, the very deliberations of the *Sobor* would be made known to King Sigismund. No, the nation had no wish to see a traitor's son ascend the throne.

More candles were lit. From their bench the sponsors of the young Romanov looked up and down the ranks of the representatives. Some protests had been expected. Yet, earlier, the vast Assembly had not shown a flicker of interest upon hearing the old and noble names of likely candidates. The story about Philaret had obviously disturbed the hierarchy. But so far those of lesser rank, both urban and rural, had not raised a single protest.

One of the sponsors reminded the Assembly of the late Czarina Anastasia, a Romanov by birth. Another pointed out that young Michael would be surrounded by wise counselors. A third asked the representatives what particular name they had in mind as an alternative. Both argument and question fell into a pool of uneasy silence. Then a tattered young man shouted that they had come together to choose a czar and not to buy a dozen heifers at a cattle fair.

"Say nay if you so wish, but give a good reason for it."

But the dissenters still refused to commit themselves. When someone asked the young Romanov's whereabouts and was told that nobody knew, there were jeers and taunts.

"Eating roast goose with his father in Kracow most likely."

The hierarchy frowned at the unsuitable levity. But those jeers ended with a play into the sponsors' hands. When at the close of the *Sobor*, votes were counted, young Romanov was elected czar. The majority could not be called overwhelming, but it more than satisfied the sponsors' expectations. The senior Archbishop gave a blessing and confirmed the election "by the will of the people," since such was the traditional formula. The *Sobor* dispersed. Pozharsky, Kuzma Minin, and a few others turned to the immediate task of tracing the young Czar's whereabouts.

Chapter XX

That great *Sobor* of 1613 was certainly a hall-mark: the crown became elective, but only conditionally so. The end of the ancient Rurik dynasty had indeed led to two earlier elections, but Boris Godunov had become czar by the will of the Moscow military and the mob, and Vassily Shuyskie had been chosen by the Duma. The end of the *Smuta*, however, had led to a striking change in the national climate. The *Sobor* being a fully representative assembly, national wishes had been consulted, an accomplishment impossible to imagine during the reigns of Ivan the Terrible and his predecessors. Democracy had risen, spoken its will, and turned back to autocracy, for the first Romanov sovereign would rule as a *samodérzhetz*, an autocrat. Muscovy had no other idea of sovereignty and the people would have been bewildered if a czar-elect were to be governed by apron strings, controlled by the nobility. Yet, however briefly, the consciousness of a link between Michael Romanov and themselves had entered the minds of the unlettered folk. Both in the cities and in the country the people were proud of the achievement in Moscow. First, a prince and a butcher had entered into as close an alliance as was possible. Too, a vast assembly had come together where even men whose right hand would not have known how to hold a quill had been invited to choose a ruler. Finally, the Czarelect came from a family that was interested in the peasantry as well as in the higher social classes. Even peasants who had never seen Moscow felt that they had—however vicariously—a share in the most momentous affair of their generation.

"Come spring, all hands to the plow and the harrow."

From Archangel in the far north to the shores of the Caspian Sea in the south there was a surge of energy despite the enormous task facing the nation. Muscovy, deeply wounded a little while before, lay scarred from end to end. The ravages of fire, violence, invasion, and chaos demanded remedies not dispensed by formal directives but by thousands of willing hands. Thus, a half-blind peasant from a village near Kostroma might say to his married son: "Go and mend your wife's spinning wheel. I reckon the young Czar would rather not see his people in tatters."

Michael Romanov, though unknown, was their

czar, and they were his people, even if he never saw the new shirt on a Kostroma peasant's back.

Trade, however, could not be repaired as quickly as a broken spinning wheel. Commerce demanded a balance between exports and imports, and what exports could a ravaged country offer? Here a venture started under Ivan the Terrible brought high dividends. Many decades had passed since the enterprising merchant family of the Strogonovs had crossed the Urals into the vast unknown country of Eastern Siberia, immensely wealthy in timber, hides, ore, and precious stones. The settlements founded by the Strogonovs had had a thin time of it during the *Smuta*. There could have been no question of sending valuable raw materials across the Ural Mountains into a country in the throes of chaos. The Strogonovs and others realized that time and care would be needed to begin sending all the hoarded treasures over the mountains. But, apart from perishable edibles, Siberia had masses of goods which, once delivered to Muscovy, would give a tremendous impetus to national trade.

The merchantry, however impoverished, pledged their daughters' dowries to pay for what timber, fish, and salt there was to export. There was an abundance of fish, but no grain or other cereals might be offered to foreign agents. Charity started at home, and Muscovy had a sharp need for many kinds of it. At Vologda, the widow of the local governor came upon a priceless cache hidden behind the orchard, and used it to buy seed, which she distributed among the villages that most needed help. Two small coffers full of silver coins and pearls the lady sent to Prince Pozharsky. "For the Czar's needs," ran her message.

Narva no longer belonged to Muscovy, but Archangel on the White Sea stirred into life once the ice had gone. Ships from England, Denmark, and the Low Countries began casting anchor along its docks. It is true that at first they did not come in great numbers, the Dutch in particular being skeptical about the improvement in conditions in Muscovy. Yet trickle by trickle, step by step, Muscovite trade began regaining its earlier health.

Meanwhile, Michael Romanov was traced by special units sent from Moscow. Formally elected czar in February 1613, he was not found for another month. Peasants led the messengers from Moscow to him, and a peasant was to save his life.

Chapter XXI

Who were the Romanovs? They were an old and highly respected family of pure Rus blood. But they were not descendants of Rurik, bore no title, and the nobility regarded them with some contempt. From father to son, from uncle to nephew, the family minded their own concerns, joined no factions, stayed out of conspiracies, and their daughters did not marry into the nobility. Some members of the family lived in Moscow. Others preferred their country manors. They made exemplary landowners, and when necessity called for it, they rode to war against Sweden, Lithuania, and Poland.

They had one distinguished trait in common. Deeply pious and true Muscovites that they were, the Romanovs were liberal and world-oriented. When Ivan III took a Paleologue girl for his bride and a group of exiled Greek scholars followed her to Moscow,

the scholars were made most welcome at the Romanov houses. The first printing presses established in the capital had Romanovs as their best customers. The Romanov mansions had more than jeweled ikons, silver and gold plate, and rare rugs in their parlors. The Romanovs had books—in manuscript and printed. Their young men knew Latin and Greek, and they had tutors from the foreign quarter to teach them geography and mathematics. The first globe in Moscow was honorably housed in a Romanov mansion.

But the Romanovs never pushed themselves into the Kremlin limelight. The occasional taunts of the titled nobility left them undisturbed. On some occa-

126

sions an overzealous bishop or abbot would cast suspicions on the Romanov "modernity." But all suspicions died as soon as they were uttered. No Romanov was ever known to break bread under a foreign roof. No Romanov ever transgressed the Church laws on fasting and abstinence. No episcopal spy ever found a roast pig on a Romanov table at a time when meat was forbidden.

The betrothal of Ivan IV to Anastasia, daughter of one Nikita Romanov, had led to many an anxious flutter among the nobility. For the first czar to marry a commoner's daughter would have been a joke if it were not an insult, the boyars had said to one another. And whoever had heard of the girl? Her parents, it was freely rumored, could not even afford a mansion in Moscow. They lived in the country, and the Czar's bride-elect would probably be good only at milking cows and feeding poultry. And she came from a numerous family. Uncles, cousins, and the rest would be certain to swarm all over the Kremlin—by virtue of a Romanov being Czarina. Petty rivalries set aside, the proud descendants of Rurik had made a common cause.

Their anxieties had been unfounded. Anastasia, once she was the Czarina, asked for no favors. Neither politics nor economics concerned her. She bore Ivan's children and spent her leisure in helping "the poor and prisoners." Gossiping observers could report only one instance of a disagreement between husband and wife, and that story was most likely born out of someone's imagination.

Among the numberless presents the Czar showered

on his wife was a fabulous necklace of rubies and diamonds sent by the Shah of Persia to Ivan on his coming-of-age. Anastasia, having heard of a disastrous famine that had befallen four villages near Tver, handed the necklace to an honest courtier, asking him to sell it and to use the proceeds for the relief of the sufferers. The story may or may not be true: it is certainly in character. Czar Ivan, riding out of Moscow on his numerous campaigns, would remark that he was leaving his Czarina to "her works of benevolence."

It was because of her acts of charity that the Romanov name had come to be grafted in the people's hearts. The whole of Muscovy had known of the Czarina's tender but firm influence over the irascible Czar. Had Anastasia not died, and at so early an age, there might never have been any *oprichnyki* and the heir to the throne probably would not have been killed by his own father.

Czar Fedor had held his mother's kin in respect and affection, and Boris Godunov may well have wondered if his brother-in-law, childless and ailing, would not name a Romanov as his successor. But Fedor had died leaving no successor.

Two years later, the upstart Czar Boris would have seen treason in a fly dropping into his goblet of wine. His spies lost no opportunity to report one case of *izména* (treason, sedition) after another. The nobility had been the first to suffer. Some were exiled, others went to the block. Wholly unfounded suspicion then had fallen on Fedor Romanov, who lived with his wife and child in Moscow. Fedor Romanov, urged the spies, was meddling in *izmena*, for all his outward modesty and quiet way of life. He was well educated, he spoke several languages, and was known to have many friends among the Dutch and English in the foreign quarter on the banks of the Yauza. There were more books than ikons in his house. It would not do to send Fedor Romanov and his wife into exile: the man was clever enough to brew a barrelful of mischief. Should the two be handed over to the hangman, and their child too, for good measure?

Boris had hesitated. In the end, husband and wife had been torn from each other. Fedor, sent under guard to a remote northern monastery, had been forcibly made a monk and given the name of Philaret. The wife had been sent to a convent well south of Moscow and had her name changed to Marfa. The question of what to do with the son, a delicate child not quite three years old, taxed the Czar.

"Let him go with his mother," Boris had decided. "So frail a child is unlikely to live long."

But Fedor Romanov's son had lived. In 1613 he was still with his mother at the Ipatiev Convent near Kostroma. He did not know that on a February day in 1613 a great Assembly in faraway Moscow had elected him czar.

That year, winter held stubbornly on in Muscovy. Not until March, with the rivers still frozen and the forests covered in snow, were Michael's whereabouts discovered and an embassy dispatched to the Ipatiev Convent.

129

Chapter XXII

The rumors about the Polish danger which had disturbed the *Sobor* in Moscow were not fantastic stories invented by ill-wishers to wreck the Assembly. There *were* spies in Moscow, and not all of them were caught.

Scant and broken though Muscovy's communication with the West was during the years of the *Smuta*, the country was not wholly isolated. The matter of the Pan-Slavic union could not fail to attract the notice of the West. Some saw in it a move toward order, the undeniable Polish culture smoothing the roughness of the Muscovite leaven, much of which had been inherited from the Tartars. Others, in particular great leaders in France and Germany, considered the plan in terms of possible military aggression against the West. The dawn of the chaotic *Smuta* certainly discomfited the Western merchants, since no trade was possible under such conditions. If the Muscovites suffered one hardship after another, the English, the Dutch, and the Flemish, to say nothing of the others, were certainly disturbed by the scarcity of entries in their ledgers, for Muscovy had been a profitable customer in the past.

Then the international grapevine heard of the victorious march on Moscow, of the shattering rout of the Poles and the preparations for the National Assembly. Not every link having been severed with the West, news and rumors from Muscovy seeped out here and there. The decision of the *Sobor* concerned foreigners inasmuch as there would be a sovereign, a government, some measure of order, and less danger that casks of Rhenish wine and bales of Flemish linen would fall into brigands' hands.

"The Czar-elect is a commoner, Michael Romanov by name," wrote a Dutch glazier from the foreign quarter in Moscow.

Well, the Low Countries and their neighbors remembered that there had been another commoner, who had seldom failed in generosity toward foreign traders. Romanov? They had not heard the name, but at least it did not twist the tongue as so many Muscovite names did.

In Poland, much more was known. Michael Romanov's father was still a prisoner at Kracow. Philaret and his colleagues had not suffered many privations, but now the atmosphere changed abruptly. The Polish jailers began treating Philaret with respect bordering on servility. Even the flunkies, waiting at table, bent their knee when serving him. What visitors he had were announced with a ceremonial a prisoner could hardly expect. His every need was anticipated. Were there enough coverlets on the Patriarch's bed? Did he get that book by John Damascene? Did the cooks remember to serve saffron sauce with the meat at the Patriarch's dinner? Was there anything else he wished?

"Liberty," Philaret might have replied, but astute statesman that he was, he merely thanked the Poles for their courtesy. He knew that neither they nor King Sigismund would tell him news of his country. The imprisonment—for all the velvet curtains and silver lamps—retained its rigidity. Early in his confinement Philaret had heard that the Poles held Moscow. Even the servants had bragged loudly in the passage outside about the White Eagle banners flying over the Kremlin towers.

Then the bragging had stopped. Philaret knew nothing about Prince Pozharsky's army, the deliverance of Muscovy, the *Sobor* election of his son, whom he had not seen for thirteen years.

King Sigismund, of course, knew everything. Pozharsky's victory over an apparently invincible Polish army was much more than a military triumph. The victory meant a miraculous heightening of morale throughout the length and breadth of Muscovy. Muscovite armies might not always be victorious in the future, but that intangible quality which came to life during the National Assembly would present serious difficulties to any plan for a future invasion.

The King thought of his distinguished prisoner, sent to Kracow originally to offer the crown of Muscovy to his son. Sigismund, determined to win that crown for himself, had imprisoned the whole embassy. The King knew that no Duma in that newly reborn country would now dream of electing a foreigner czar.

Philaret had been a prisoner of note. He was much more than that now and the King saw in him a most valuable hostage, though there is no written evidence of the possible part played by the King in the plot that was to form against the life of the young Czar-elect. The King certainly had a number of well-trained spies in Moscow, and they kept in touch with their compatriots on the eastern border of Poland.

When the Muscovite leaders discovered the whereabouts of Michael Romanov, they organized an embassy to ride to Kostroma. The information, however, had reached the Polish spies a few days earlier. An Orthodox convent housing a handful of frightened Muscovite nuns and the delicate lad of sixteen! Such an easy adventure was hardly in accord with the Poles' mettle. Yet they had gauged the result. The boy's name had already become a clarion call in the country. For all the Poles knew, some news of the election had already reached as far as Kostroma, but since everybody in the country firmly believed that Muscovy was cleared of Poles, it was unlikely that guards would be on duty near the convent. Killing the boy would kill the resurgence in the land, thus paving the way for another invasion from Poland.

Seven Polish knights were involved; they saw themselves as singularly honored by their King. That much belongs to recorded history. The framework to follow has been created by poets, musicians, painters, and sculptors of later centuries, men to whom the name Romanov meant as much as it had meant to Muscovy in 1613.

But the framework is not based on wild fantasy. The background of the story is true to the least detail.

Chapter XXIII

Heavily cloaked and fully armed, the seven Polish noblemen, their attendants and spare horses following them, decided to ride into the heart of thickly forested Kostroma lands. The seven had made a plan: they would come to the Ipatiev Convent as friends of Patriarch Philaret, and deliver a false message to the young Czar-elect. His father, yearning to be united to his son, asked the boy to trust the messengers to bring him safely to Kracow.

But the supposedly infallible grapevine stumbled rather badly on this occasion, the spies having failed to send reports of the latest developments in Muscovy. The Polish knights started on their ride quite unaware that by then there was hardly a peasant household around Kostroma that had not heard about the National Assembly. Nor did the Poles realize that the Romanov mother and son had lived among these people for thirteen years and had endeared themselves to the neighborhood with their patience, kindness, and humility. The Polish knights were fortunate in finding a guide, a young man of Polish stock but born in Muscovy. No open roads could serve the conspirators' purpose. They needed a guide to lead them through the western border of Muscovy into the immense forests girdling Kostroma. At night they sheltered in isolated huts, the attendants killing the inhabitants to avoid the risk of betrayal.

A brief winter day was ending when the conspirators were caught in a wide glade by a blizzard. They reined in and peered ahead, but the snowstorm had wiped out every landmark. Once its fury had abated, the conspirators could see a long, low, timbered building to the left of them and a twisting narrow path ahead, with a flicker of light at the end of it. The Poles dismounted and made for the shed. It was deserted.

The Poles ordered the grooms to fetch some kindling for a fire in the shed. The men came back with some logs and a piece of shattering news: they had come on the guide's body under a huge limb of a tree felled in the storm. The conspirators stared at one another. In the dim lantern light their faces looked ashen. They were lost in a forest they did not know. The breaking of dawn would hardly help them. They swore and stamped their feet until a groom reported that the light still burned at the end of the path, and they decided that it was most likely some forester's

136

hut. They would not kill the man but make him lead them to the convent gates; their guide had told them they were not far.

No horse could have been ridden down that path, and the conspirators decided to walk, leaving the grooms and the mounts behind in the shed. The seven men, gauntleted hands on their swords, struggled through the thick carpet of snow. They reached the hut, its flicker of rush light coming through a tiny window. The leader knocked, and an elderly peasant opened the creaking door. The hut was so small that the seven Poles crowded it. By a narrow trestle a young girl and a lad were getting a meal together. They raised their heads and stared. The peasant slammed the door and watched the visitors in silence.

They had lost their guide in a blizzard, explained the Pole, and left their grooms and horses in a deserted shed in a glade behind. They were on their way to the Ipatiev Convent. Prince Pozharsky and other noblemen in Moscow knew about it. They were carrying a message from Patriarch Philaret to the young Czar.

At these words, the girl gripped the edge of the trestle and the boy's eyes widened. Their father bowed and continued stroking his beard. An illiterate peasant though he was, he knew that his people in Moscow would never have sent one Pole, let alone a group of them, with any messages.

Ivan Soussanin, a widower, was a forester. The Ipatiev Convent walls were just beyond a wide clump of firs behind the hut. Soussanin had been at the convent earlier that day and had heard that an embassy from the *Sobor* in Moscow would reach Kostroma within two or three days. To Soussanin, the vast forests of the neighborhood were all as familiar as his own back yard. When another Pole remarked that he would be well rewarded for his trouble, the peasant bowed again. Yes, he knew a short cut to the convent, but even so, it was some distance from the hut. Would the gentlemen honor him by sharing some cabbage broth and a loaf? Their leader replied haughtily. Their grooms had already served them supper and they were in a hurry to deliver their message.

Soussanin got into his warm clothes, filled a lantern with oil, blessed his son and daughter, and moved to the door, the Poles following him. When the door was slammed behind the last unwanted visitor, brother and sister flew to each other's arms. Both knew that no Pole could be a friend to a Muscovite.

Soussanin led the way through a fairly easy glade to the right of the hut, turned left, and reached an immense forest as the March wind moaned overhead. The Poles followed, often losing their foothold in the deep, wet snow. The wind dropped. There was not a sound to be heard. Soussanin marched on. They left the forest for a stretch of rough common and were just about to cross it when the world became eerily silver. In the moonlight the Poles saw a great forest stretching into apparent infinity. In between the huge trunks of the trees the snow lay in drifts.

Soussanin marched on, the snow sometimes up to his waist. Now and again the moon slid behind a cloud, and the world would have been wholly dark had it not been for the peasant's oil lantern.

Behind him, the seven nobles began muttering oaths in their own tongue. Unaccustomed to such a hard, long tramp, they were growing tired. They could not gauge the time they had spent in the woods, but the peasant's "short cut" now aroused their suspicions. The Poles knew the poverty of the peasants in Muscovy, and they had promised ten gold pieces to their guide. So where was the convent?

The terrible wood widened into a glade, moonlight dancing and glancing across it. An owl screeched and was answered by another. Soussanin stopped and turned to face the Poles. Their patience in shreds, they must have asked him how far they were from the convent. He may have told them that they were a great distance from it. He may have said that they would never find their own way back. But there were no witnesses to record those stirring moments. Three days later, searchers from the neighboring villages came upon Soussanin's body hacked by Polish swords, and carried it back to render it the final honors. Not one Pole escaped from those woods.

Soussanin's murder came as a fitting postscript to the Moscow *Sobor*'s announcement. "By the will of the people." It is most unlikely that any humble forester had ever spoken to Michael Romanov, but the idea of unity, however inarticulate, was firmly lodged

in the peasant mind. That unity depended on a czar of pure Muscovite stock, someone uncommitted to factions and rivalries, someone brought up in the tenets of the Orthodox faith, one who was closely acquainted with the national needs, who would know how to relieve the people's misery. The unlettered peasant Soussanin became a symbol of loyalty, steadfastness, simplicity. The conspiracy had been shamelessly and rather absurdly contrived by the Poles. Soussanin had contrived nothing. Determined to save the boy's life, he had never considered the consequences. Poor and unknown, that peasant should not be regarded in terms

140

of individual heroism alone. Rather, he stands as a symbol of Muscovy, urban and rural, zealous for the unity so hardily acquired in the early seventeenth century. Had anyone asked Soussanin if he loved his country, he would have been bewildered by the question. He and his country were one—but he would not delve into such things. He saw it all not as a problem to be solved but as a necessity to accept. In that simple unlettered peasant beat a heart which, all unknown to him, was in keeping with the early Kievan Rus, Rus under the Tartar yoke, Muscovy.

Soussanin's death in the remote Kostroma forest was the new young dynasty's most proud signature. His son and daughter, to their last descendants through three centuries to come, would be showered with tokens of appreciation. Yet these were accidentals. The focal point lay elsewhere, and it proved to Muscovy that in spite of all the dissensions at the *Sobor*, young Michael Romanov was an honestly elected sovereign.

Little wonder that two centuries later poets, composers, sculptors, and painters of Soussanin's country felt the theme in their pulses.

Index

Adashev, 37, 40, 51
Anastasia Romanova, 36–9, 45, 49–52, 57, 71, 119, 127–8
Archangel, 124
Astrakhan, 14, 38, 65, 96

Baltic Sea, 13, 39, 40, 56–8
Basmanov, 53
Black Sea, 13

Caspian Sea, 14, 38–9, 43
Chancellor, Richard, 58
Charles V, 40

Chudov Abbey, 105, 107, 114

Dimitry (son of Ivan IV and Anastasia), 39, 43, 49
Dimitry (son of Ivan IV and Maria Nagaya), 59, 62, 64–5
Dimitry the Pretender, 73–85, 88–9, 100
Donskoy, Dimitry, 7, 39
Duma: election of Boris, 67; and Fedor, 61, 63–4; and Ivan IV, 23, 36, 45; and the Pretender,

Duma (*cont.*)
77, 91; and Vassily,
95–7, 121; war with
Sigismund, 100–1,
104, 106, 133

Edward VI, 58
Elena Glynskaya, 15–16,
18–19
Elizabeth Tudor, 58–9,
61

Fedor, 49, 51–2, 56, 59,
61–3, 65–6, 71, 128

George, Prince, 15, 19–
21
Godunov, Boris: and
Fedor, 61–4, 66–8,
128; and Ivan IV, 57,
59, 60; reign of, 69–
71, 73–7, 121, 128–9
Godunov, Fedor, 71, 77
Godunov, Irina, 57, 59,
61–3, 65, 67–8
Godunov, Xenia, 69, 77

Hastings, Mary, 59
Hermogen, Patriarch,
105–10, 114

Iona, Metropolitan, 67,
69
Ipatiev Convent, 129,
135, 137
Ivan III, 8, 12, 14–15,
42, 125
Ivan IV, 71–3, 75, 77,
81, 83, 88, 91, 93,
100, 121, 123; and
Boris Godunov, 57;
childhood of, 15–24;
death of, 60–2; foreign
affairs of, 38–41, 44–
5, 58–60; killing of
Ivan the Younger, 54;
and Anastasia, 36–7,
49–51, 127–8; suspi-
cion of aristocracy, 52–
4; Tartar war, 57
Ivan the Younger, 49–52,
54–5

Johan of Denmark, 69

Kazan, 14, 38–9, 57, 65, 96
Kazan, Khan of, 18, 38
Khan Batiy, 7
Kholmogory, 43
Kiev, 5, 6, 8, 9
Kostroma, 129, 133, 135–6, 138, 141
Kracow, 82, 100–1, 104, 118–19, 131, 133, 135
Kulikovo, 7
Kurbsky, Andrey, 51, 54

Maria Nagaya, 59, 62, 72, 83, 92–3
Miloslavsky, Danila, 89
Minin, Kuzma, 100–11, 114–16, 120
Mnishek, Marina, 73, 81, 83, 88, 91–3, 100–1
Mnishek, Prince, 73, 81–3, 88, 91
Moscow: defense of, 96–7, 101–4, 130, 132; dominance of Muscovy, 8, 9, 12; freed from Tartars, 7; life under Ivan IV, 25–30, 45–6; during reign of Boris, 70, 76–7; during reign of Dimitry, 88; rescue of, 110, 112–15, 131; and the Romanovs, 125–9, 138–9; threatened by Tartars, 57; as a trade center, 42
Moskva River, 45, 94, 109

Narva, 41, 58, 124
National Assembly, 116–21, 129–32, 135, 138–9, 141
Nijny-Novgorod, 109–11, 116
Novgorod, 5, 7, 8, 42–3, 54, 102

Oprichnyki, 53–4, 57, 60, 128

Philaret, see Romanov, Fedor

Philip, Metropolitan, 54
Pozharsky, Prince, 110–12, 114–17, 120, 124, 132, 137
Pskov, 5, 7, 67, 95

Romanov family, 71, 79, 125–8, 134
Romanov, Fedor, 72, 101, 118–19, 128–9, 131–2, 135, 137
Romanov, Marfa, 128–9, 135–6
Romanov, Michael, 72, 118–24, 129, 131–3, 135–7, 139–41
Romanov, Nikita, 127
Rurik, House of, 5–8, 18, 36, 65, 71, 75, 104, 117, 121, 125
Rus, 4–8, 65, 125, 141

Serebrianin, Prince, 51
Sevsk, 75
Shuyskie, Ivan, 18–19, 21
Shuyskie princes, 18, 20–2

Shuyskie, Vassily, 65, 77, *see also* Vassily, Czar
Siberia, 44, 123
Sigismund, King, 82, 88, 96–7, 99, 101–4, 118, 132–4
Skuratin, 53–4
Smolensk, 67, 96–7
Smuta, 77, 110, 121, 123, 130
Sobor, see National Assembly
Soussanin, Ivan, 137–41
Stararussa, 43
Strogonov family, 44–5, 56, 123
Suleiman II, 57
Sylvester, 37, 51

Tartars: Crimean, 14, 18, 38, 51, 57, 65, 99; early domination of Rus, 7, 39; influence on Muscovy life, 8, 9, 12
Terem, 9, 10, 45–6
Tula, 43
Tver, 30, 33, 95, 118

Uglich, 62, 64–5, 73, 81, 83, 93

Vassily, Czar, 95–6, 121; *see also* Shuyskie, Vassily
Vassily, Prince, 14–15, 17, 19
Viazma, 42
Vladimir of Kiev, 5
Volga River, 14, 18, 38, 109

Vologda, 87, 123

White Sea, 14, 58, 124
Wladislas, Prince, 99–101, 118, 133

Yauza River, 45, 109, 129

Znakhár, 10–11, 33
Zoë Paleologue, 14

E. M. Almedingen, who died in 1971 in Bath, England, was born in St. Petersburg in 1898 into one of Russia's leading aristocratic-intellectual families. Miss Almedingen studied at the University of Petrograd and later taught English medieval history and literature there. She had made her home in England since 1922. In 1950 she was named a Fellow of the Royal Society of Literature in Great Britain.

Many of Miss Almedingen's books have been published in the United States, including her autobiography, *Tomorrow Will Come*, winner of the Atlantic Monthly Prize, published in 1941 and reissued in 1968. She is also the author of *The Romanovs* and *Saint Francis of Assisi*. Among her books for children are *Katia* (1967), *Young Mark* (1968), *A Candle at Dusk* (1969), *Fanny* (1970), *Ellen* (1970), and *Anna* (1972).